The Good Book
& *a glass of sweet tea*

Vicki E. Gambill

Vicki Elliott Gambill

The Good Book
a glass of sweet tea

TATE PUBLISHING & *Enterprises*

Published by Tate Publishing & Enterprises, LLC
127 E. Trade Center Terrace | Mustang, Oklahoma 73064 USA
1.888.361.9473 | www.tatepublishing.com

Tate Publishing is committed to excellence in the publishing industry. The company reflects the philosophy established by the founders, based on Psalm 68:11,
"The Lord gave the word and great was the company of those who published it."

Book design copyright © 2010 by Tate Publishing, LLC. All rights reserved.
Cover design by Brandon Wood
Interior design by Joey Garrett

Published in the United States of America

ISBN: 978-1-61566-601-0
1. Religion / Christian Life / Inspirational
2. Religion / Christian Life / Spiritual Growth
10.01.19

To the glory of my heavenly Father and to honor my mom and dad, Janie and Stokey Elliott.

Acknowledgments

There are so many deserving of my gratitude for contributing to this journey. First and foremost is God. His never-ending patience, grace, blessings, and mercy on such a late bloomer are simply beyond words. Every breath I take is cause for gratitude.

John and Tait are my two most precious and cherished gifts from God. John has worked tirelessly not only to support us literally but emotionally as well, affording me the opportunity to devote myself to all my new endeavors over the last few years. John, you are truly the love of life. God blessed me the day he brought us together, and I look forward to growing old with you by my side. Tait, my baby, my miracle, and God's special gift, to watch you grow over the years and become the beautiful young woman you are today has been my pleasure, even with the addition of a few gray hairs. Your smile warms my heart, and your sparkling blue eyes reflect the beauty of your soul.

My family, talk about the formative years! Where would I be without their influence? The good, the bad, and the ugly—they were there through them all. They protected, loved, and helped mold me into the woman I am today.

My friends, my prayer warriors, and sister-girls, thank you for holding me up when I could not stand.

There were many others throughout my life too numerous to mention. You will get to know some of them as you read.

Table of Contents

Foreword

There are times in our lives when God sends someone to bless us, teach us, or encourage us. Little did I know several years ago that he was going to do that for me through Vicki Gambill. A quiet, reserved woman I had never seen before walked into our Wednesday night Bible study. We worshiped at the same church, but we were in different services, so our paths had never crossed. Because of her quiet nature, Vicki never talked much in class; however, it did not take me long to learn that when she did speak, I would listen. Her words were always thoughtful and full of wisdom and grace, and I always found myself thinking about her comments long after class was over. Since that first night, our relationship has grown and changed, and I am blessed to call Vicki my sister and my mentor.

It is truly an honor and a privilege to introduce you to Vicki and her book. I believe that Vicki has written this book in such a way that you can read straight through and travel along with her on her journey, or you can pick out a specific chapter that resonates with where you are currently in your life and share in what God has taught her. Vicki has honestly opened up her life to us and shown us how God has taken every experience, circumstance, and difficulty and woven them together into the beautiful tapestry of her life.

It was rather ironic that when Vicki asked me to read her manuscript, I had just reentered the corporate world, and I was reading about her leaving the corporate world. Her child had gone off to college, and I still have children in grade school. I share this because even though our lives are at very different stages, her words spoke to me and taught me, and she challenged me in many different areas of my faith. No matter what stage of your life you are in at this moment, this book will speak to you. If we are not in a certain stage, we can be certain that we will be one day.

First Corinthians 10:31 says, "Whatever you do, do it for the glory of the Lord." Vicki is glorifying God in every aspect of her life, even her past. It is a beautiful thing to see God redeem our pasts and make something beautiful out of them. I pray God will use this book to speak to you at this very moment in your life, and I pray that you will feel the love of Christ enveloping you as you read through these pages and are blessed by them.

—Gay G. Dempsey

Introduction

After spending more than twenty-five years in corporate America and picking up many of its ruthless, ugly traits along the way, I didn't like the person I had become. So I packed that baggage away and embarked on an amazing new journey of spiritual and self-exploration.

Almost seven years have passed since making that decision. And much like a caterpillar leaving the cocoon, I have become a new creature, emerging and growing each and every day. How this metamorphosis occurred was the direct result of God's amazing grace. Through his many teachings, I learned a much more rewarding way of living. You've heard that God works in mysterious ways; well, as you read, you will see firsthand the results through the many facets of my life.

God! That's where it all begins. In reality, he had been there waiting all along. I just wasn't receptive. When I started pursuing him, amazing things began to happen. The many incomprehensible chapters of my life began to make sense. Things I had never understood before finally revealed their hidden meanings. He helped me see parts of myself that had been buried for years and helped me develop whole new characteristics that I would have never imagined.

Some of the twists and turns on my journey have been, to say the least, monumental, and at times devastating. I think when you read these circumstances some of you will be quite capable of relating. Hopefully, you may gain some insight that could be beneficial. My prayer is that God will use my examples as a vehicle to help heal hurting hearts and bring peace and comfort to those who seek him; and maybe even help a few more folks out there find their way to a love they will never find anywhere else.

As my writing continued, I remembered a deep desire from way back in my college days. For some strange reason, I wanted to publish a book someday. Now, folks, that's a pretty big dream for a small-town Tennessee girl. I didn't understand why I felt that way either because I certainly wasn't a journalism major or in any other related field, for that matter. So as the years passed and I pursued other interests, that desire was long forgotten. But all of a sudden, here it was emerging once again, out of nowhere. Do you think that could be destiny? Perhaps!

Then again, as I was writing about my mother's difficult childhood, I recalled something I heard her say on many occasions. *Somebody needs to write a book and tell our story.* Little did she know that many, many years later, that seed she planted would take root. I do believe this book is the direct result of that seed.

Before my journey, I would never have recognized things like destiny and seeds. I have learned many new concepts on this amazing quest. And this is my humble attempt to share those details with you.

The Decision

Launch out into the deep, and let down your nets
for a draught.

Luke 5:4

H ere we were at a crossroads. The company
I had worked for the past eleven years was
suddenly included in a corporate bankruptcy
filing. Severe layoffs ensued. All of a sudden I found
myself unemployed. Little did I realize at the time, the
door that had slammed shut in my face would lead to
an even bigger door of opportunity that would prove to
be much more beneficial in the long run. But that was
yet to be seen!

What to do? What to do? That was the big question.
After recovering from the initial shock and the blow
to my ego, I came to the realization that the reflection I saw in the mirror wasn't very comforting. I saw
an angry, unhappy woman and wondered why I hadn't
noticed that before. Where did I go? How did I get so
lost along the way? These were the burning questions,
and I knew I would not find the answers this time in
my usual manner. I finally realized my success in the
working world had nothing to do with *the real me*. I
needed a change of substantial magnitude.

Our daughter was soon to become a teenager. After
spending all those years in corporate America, my husband and I decided it was a good time for me to be at
home more for her all too unpredictable years. I had

tried this role once before when she was born. I didn't last long, though; just a few months passed before I decided I needed adult conversation as well. I suppose that was one of those *right timing* issues we have in life.

This time seemed different somehow. I just had this sense it was what I needed to do at this juncture in my life. So I decided to stay home, and my husband stood steadfast in support of me.

He has always been my biggest supporter, no matter what the issue. And trust me, this was a huge issue. We aren't rich by any means, and for me to stop working was going to require a major lifestyle adjustment. As much as I had grown to detest corporate America, I did like my paycheck.

So, we bit the bullet and just did it. I'm by no means suggesting this is what everyone should do. In fact, I know there are some of you who couldn't possibly consider this choice and others who simply wouldn't want to. It has, however, been a good decision for our family. It hasn't been without many concessions, though. We don't eat out most nights like we used to. Now we have dinner together as a family every evening. It's amazing what you learn about each other when you just sit down together for a meal. You can do that and still work.

I'm sure I don't have to tell you that my wardrobe isn't what it used to be either. Blue jeans are mostly the attire of choice. You wouldn't believe the money you save on this one item alone—provided you don't have a taste for those expensive designer jeans all the celebrities wear. Let's be realistic here, girls! Who looks like that anyway? I know my physique doesn't quite scream *movie star.*

We also had to change the kinds of vacations we took. They sometimes became shorter in length and distance. My mom would call that *trimming the fat.* It's amazing what you can find in your own backyard with a little creative exploration. For instance, Nashville has much more to offer than just country music. We have also been known to vacation at home from time to time. I really enjoy the no-packing aspect of that one.

Giving up material things wasn't as big of an adjustment for me as the mental concessions were. It took me a long time to get used to the fact that there was only one paycheck, and what if something happened and we lost it? God forbid! I have, however, come to the conclusion that you can't base your life on *what if.* Think about it—what a gloom and doom outlook.

I don't believe God put us on this earth to live life expecting the worst all the time. I believe he loves us and wants us to be successful and happy. I heard an old saying a long time ago that made a big impression on me, and I've never forgotten it. *Yesterday is gone. Tomorrow isn't here yet (or promised, for that fact), but today is a present.* The Bible also teaches this concept: "This is the day which the Lord hath made; we will rejoice and be glad in it" (Psalm 118:24).

Now, I know you're thinking all of that still wouldn't make up for the loss in salary, and you're exactly right. These were just a few of the changes we had to make in order to achieve our goal. The decision to live on one income is an absolute rearrangement of your lifestyle and mindset. I might add here, it was one of toughest decisions we had ever made in our entire married life—so far!

Let's get back to one of my reasons for staying home in the first place. You know, it's funny; most folks seem to think the most important time to be around for your kids is when they are very young. That is an important stage in their development. Not many parents want to miss their child's first steps or any of the other firsts that come along, for that matter. Sometimes life just necessitates different priorities, and being there isn't always possible. So we all just have to do the best we can and learn to live with the choices we make.

All too often I think the older kids get overlooked. Let me tell you, folks; you think it's tough when your kids are small. Just wait. My poppa used to say—and I never understood it until now—*When your kids are little, they step on your toes, but when they get older, they step on your heart.* Now, just how profound is that?

Yes, they're old enough to stay at home alone. But what are they doing while you're not around? You know, I remember reading that the majority of teenagers have sex between the time they get out of school and the time their parents get home from work. I have to admit, I was surprised. I thought that kind of activity would more likely take place away from home, where their prospects of being caught by a parent's or sibling's early arrival wouldn't be as great.

There isn't enough paper in the world to write about all the kids who have been solicited over the Internet. The last statistic I heard was one out of every four kids. Can you believe that? I can't stress enough how important it is for you parents to know what your kids are doing on their computers. We had an incident our-selves. It wasn't nearly as significant as being solicited, but it too got our attention.

Our daughter liked to chat with her friends online. Two boys in our neighborhood somehow figured out her ID and password, and they went online and pre-tended to be her. They said some pretty nasty things that really upset us, and this went on for months, until they eventually got bored, I suppose. Fortunately, she told us what was happening, and we kept her off the computer the entire time. So at least our inner circle of friends knew it wasn't really her. As for the others, well, they were going to think what they wanted to anyway. That was the least of our concern.

It seems this is also a pretty common problem. It's called Internet bullying, and it has been known to really cause some major problems for the victims. The bullies think it's funny. What kind of demented think-ing is that? Makes you wonder what kind of productive members of society they'll grow up to be, doesn't it?

I'm not at all surprised by some kids' behavior today. Just look at all the stuff they are exposed to. You can't watch TV anymore without seeing drugs, sex, violence, and terrible language on every channel. It is so hard for parents who are actually trying to raise their children in a positive manner to find the right tools. Let's not forget the role models out there either. It seems that all they ever show are the bad ones, like the ball players using steroids and beating up fans in the stands. Why do they get all the airtime? Ratings, that's why. More people will watch the bad stuff. I think that speaks vol-umes about our society today. Don't you?

Let's fast forward a bit. Our daughter turned sixteen and got her driver's license. Well, she hadn't been driving but a month, and we got the phone call no parent wants to get. She had been in an accident. *Thank God!* She only had a few cuts and a black eye. Her car, on the other hand, didn't fare so well. It was totaled. Parents, you don't know fear until you watch your child drive off alone for the first time. Pray, people, pray.

I asked her one day if she felt safe at school. She replied, "Yeah, why?" Well, because just that week, I had seen four different high schools on the news. Every one of them had students bringing guns to school. Besides that, this particular issue does have a significant impact on our community. Our daughter's high school happened to be one of those schools you've seen on the news.

One year, one of the students shot and killed a fellow classmate—believe it or not, over a girl! The tragic death of a fine young man was so senseless. He will never have the opportunity to grow into the man of integrity he could have become. And this all happened within a few days of graduation. The young man who did the shooting had a scholarship to college, and he would have been gone in a few months if he just hadn't let jealousy take control. Now, he's in prison. The girl—well, last I heard, she left town. The pressure was just too much. Three lives so drastically changed in the blink of an eye and with one terrible choice. The sad part is that it wasn't just those three lives. It was those three families and an entire community.

Then there's teenage pregnancy. We live in small-town USA, and when our daughter was in eighth grade, there were two pregnant girls in her class. There were only thirty eighth-grade girls in the entire school, and probably half of them hadn't even reached puberty yet. That number drastically goes up the older they get. And let's not forget all the nasty sexually transmitted diseases out there today.

What about all the drugs! They are everywhere, including in your own medicine or liquor cabinets. I assure you these kids know exactly where to find them and how to use them. I've heard too many horror stories.

Our daughter, on the other hand, would absolutely disagree with a need for guidance. They don't think they need any. They think they are ready for anything and everything that comes along. I know you can remember those self-absorbed, invincible teenage years too.

These are just a few of the issues our teenagers are dealing with today. There are many, many more. You wouldn't believe some of the things I've heard. Don't get me wrong here; we had a beautiful, good-natured, smart, loving daughter. She was also young and impressionable. That's why we thought parental guidance at this particular time for her was so very crucial, and still there is no guarantee. She would still make some of the wrong choices along the way. You can't be with them twenty-four–seven, nor should you. They have to have some freedom, or they will never mature.

My job is to make the opportunities for the wrong choices as limited, difficult, and undesirable as possible. That's why it's called parenting. Fight for your children, people. I assure you Satan is.

The Parents

A good name is rather to be chosen than great riches, and loving favor rather than silver and gold.

Proverbs 22:1

Now you know our daughter was one of the deciding factors in my decision to stop working. I also found another important one—my parents. I have to say, just in time too. I wasn't even home a year when I lost my father. I am so grateful now for those special few months we had together.

My father was much older than my mom—sixteen years, to be exact. He might have had some miles on him, but he got around better than a lot of folks half his age. In fact, he walked himself into the emergency room the day he died. I have always concluded that I wasn't exactly planned, since he was forty-five when I was born, but that's a whole different story. At least, that's what my big brother jokingly says. Ah, big brothers, aren't they sweet?

Three years before Dad died, he had a mild heart attack. The heart attack itself wasn't that big of an issue, but the other problem they found was. They found an eight-centimeter aortic aneurysm. We were all of a sudden bombarded with all kinds of doctors wanting to operate. We were at one of the best hospitals in the country, mind you, and I do believe that if anyone could have fixed the problem it would have been them, even though the oldest person they had ever success-fully done this procedure on had been in his early sev-enties, and my dad had a couple of decades on him.

As Mom, my brother, and I began contemplating what route we should take, guess who chimed in on the subject? My dad had his own very strong opinion. I suppose when you get as old as he was, you spend a lot of time thinking about those kinds of possibilities. Anyway, his statement hit me like a ton of bricks. "I want quality, not quantity." It seemed his biggest fear was to continue living in an undesirable or vegetative state.

Mother totally accepted his decision without ques-tion. I know she sort of thinks along those same lines herself. My brother, on the other hand, was leaning toward taking the chance with surgery. As for me, I thought if I insisted that he have surgery and it turned out that he was never well again, I would have a really hard time living with that outcome. On the other hand, if he didn't have the surgery he was going to die one day. Let's face it; he knew that at his age, that day wasn't that far off anyway. That is, bar none, the hardest kind of decision a family ever has to make. Folks, talk to each other so you know what your loved ones' wishes are, and then respect them. Better yet, while they are still able, get them to prepare a living will. It will save a lot of heartache when those kinds of decisions have to be made.

Needless to say, we brought him home his way. No surgery. I know a lot of people out there wouldn't agree with that choice, but hey, that's okay. I not only live with it, but it gives me comfort to know I left him his dignity. I am also happy to say that he lived three more wonderful, happy, good-quality years.

Now, I couldn't complete this part of the story without talking about the day he died. If ever God brought a peaceful death to a good Christian man, it was for my dad. I had spent the entire day before he died at his house. I mowed the grass, fixed gutters, helped him straighten a fencepost—I just did all kinds of little chores around the house. I even painted some pretty little flowers on the shed for Mom. Anyway, he didn't miss a step with me. When he got tired, he'd just drag his little chair out in the yard wherever I was working and sit there and talk and laugh with me the whole time.

The next morning when Mom got up, he told her his back was hurting. He told her it had bothered him most of the night, but he hadn't wanted to wake her. That's just the kind of man he was. She took him to the emergency room doors, and he got out of the car and walked in. By this time my husband, my brother, and I were all on the way to the hospital. When we arrived, the doctors told us the aneurysm was leaking and that it was time to life-flight him to Vanderbilt Hospital in Nashville, or it was time to say goodbye. Well, like everyone else, our first instinct was the former, but he had other plans. When we talked to him he said, "No. They aren't cutting on me, and I'm ready to go home when the good Lord is ready to take me."

Once again we reluctantly respected his wishes. Mom did, however, have one request of the doctors. She asked them to keep him as pain free as possible. They were so gentle and respectful with her. They immediately moved us to a quiet room and hooked him up with a morphine drip. My brother asked Daddy if there was anything he wanted to tell us. He said, "Yes, y'all take care of your mother. Y'all always stay together." Then he looked over at me, laughed, and said, "And you get that lawn mower fixed." He still had his sense of humor until the very end. (The mower broke the day before.) By this time, all of his grandchildren were there as well. He talked to all of them and told them he loved them, and they told him the same. We told him we loved him and that he was a great father, and he told us he loved us. Notice he didn't say we were great kids. Like I said, he had his sense of humor until the end. Then he just went to sleep, and a few hours later he was gone.

Death is never an easy thing to deal with under any circumstances, but I sure hope the good Lord sees fit to let me go home in a similar manner. I don't know, but his peaceful death might have had something to do with the kind of man he was. I could honestly fill pages telling you all kinds of great things about this simple, uneducated, hard-working, southern man, but I'll just tell you a couple of my favorite ones.

First of all in my entire life, I never once heard this man say one bad thing about another human being. I just find that phenomenal. I never saw him lose his temper. I guess my favorite example of his character is a time back when my brother and I were young and money was pretty tight. *Tight* is an understatement. We just didn't have a lot. My dad always had a huge garden. That was the major food source for our family. Dad grew the vegetables, and Mom canned them. So you can imagine how important the man's rotor tiller was to him. For all you city folk, that's a little plow. Anyway, my brother was a teenager, and there was an important dance coming up at school. Most of you are too young to remember, but back then the old white painter's pants were the fad of the day. My brother just thought he had to have a pair. Well, Mom and Dad just didn't have the extra money to buy them. So my dad disappeared for a while and went to town. It wasn't long before he came back home with a sack, and in it was a brand new pair of those pants. It wasn't until garden time that spring, when Dad was out there with his shovel and hoe, that we realized he had gone and sold his tiller to get my brother those pants. What a father!

The world today could sure use a few good fathers like him. He was a gentle, kind, yet strong, man. He wasn't very well educated and worked in a cotton mill all his life, but you know what? I loved him, and I can't tell you how proud I am to have had him as my dad. If I could make a wish for each child being born in this world today, it would be to have the pleasure of having a father figure like mine.

Now I'll tell you a little bit about my mom. She is hands down the strongest woman I have ever known or probably will ever know. The only way I can explain the strength in this tiny little woman is to go back to her roots. She was born in 1927, and I know you folks know enough about history to know those were the hardest times this nation has ever seen economically.

On top of all of that, she was the sixth baby girl in her family. No one knows what happened at birth or during the pregnancy, but her mother passed away fourteen days after she was born. At birth she only weighed two pounds, and she was born at home. Now, tell me God didn't mean for her to be on this earth. Her oldest sister, who was sixteen at the time, used to carry her around on a pillow because she was too small to hold. She told me many times that when her mother died, the doctor told her poppa there would be another one to bury before morning. Thank God he was wrong.

Poppa was a poor man. He spent his life traveling around from one cotton mill to another. Sometimes he would do some sharecropping, or just any kind of manual labor that would put food on the table. He often left the six girls alone for weeks at a time while he worked until he could save enough money to move them wherever he had managed to find a job. He somehow always found a way to keep the girls together.

She's told me about the times the younger sisters would walk along the railroad tracks and pick up pieces of coal that had fallen off the trains. That served as a crucial part of their heat source. Then they would go out in the field and pick dandelions, poke salad, or anything they could find to eat. Their poppa was a very proud man, and they were never aloud to beg or take charity. So needless to say, they survived the best way they could. She never slept in a real bed when she was a child. She called her bed an old straw tick thrown on the floor. The walls of the houses they lived in had cracks so big there was no keeping the winter chill out. I'm sure by now you get the picture.

Out of all those hard times, I think the one thing that bothers her most is the fact that she doesn't know what her mother looked like. Her explanation for that one is that her mother was of Native American descent, and they thought it was bad luck to have their picture made. So her mother literally scratched her face off every picture that had ever been taken. We have no idea what the woman looked like.

I suppose when you grow up under those kinds of circumstances, you develop either tremendous strength or extreme bitterness. I am so very thankful hers is strength. I think all those adverse conditions are what made her so fiercely loyal to her home and family. If I turn into even half the wife and mother she was, I'll consider myself successful!

She surely had to call on all of her strength when my dad died. Here she was, all of a sudden alone after being married to this man for fifty-six years. I'm sure she had mentally tried to prepare herself for his death because like I said, we had known about his condition for the past three years. You can prepare yourself all you want, but when the actual time comes, you still don't want to let them go.

She did extremely well, though! She kept right on living in Shelbyville in the house they shared for the majority of their married life. Then two years later, one day out of the blue she said, "I think I want to move to Fayetteville and get a little closer to you, but I don't want to live with you." She still wanted to have her own place. I said that would be great. In fact, it would be a lot more convenient for me because I was driving over there twice a week at the time anyway.

I do believe Mom knew her health was beginning to deteriorate. A few months earlier she'd had a scare with her heart. I think maybe that was the trigger. She realized she was living in Shelbyville alone. My brother lives in Franklin, which is right outside of Nashville, and my home is in Fayetteville, Tennessee. So I immediately began to look for her a place to live.

She didn't want another house because she didn't want all of those responsibilities anymore. Her idea was to simplify. We were fortunate to get an apartment in a nice little retirement community. I know in my heart that divine intervention played a huge part in the timing and availability of the home we found for her because we were able to get her a place within just a couple of months. The puzzle pieces just fell into place. That's what you call some of God's holy ease.

It was, however, very difficult to sell their home. She was her usual mountain of strength and logic through the entire process. She kept the furniture and things she wanted for her apartment, and then she gave the family anything they wanted. Everything else was put in a yard sale or given away. I can't imagine how she felt watching her entire life's worth just disappear. I know it sure tugged at my heart knowing that this was the place my brother and I grew up, and now it was gone.

I will never forget what she told the man who bought the house the day we closed the deal. She said, "I hope you are as happy there as we have been for the last forty-three years." Now that's a generous heart. Most people would have been thinking about themselves and what they had given up, not the happiness of the person taking over their home.

Well, she had only been living in her new home for eight months when I called her one morning and knew something just wasn't right. She was coherent, but it seemed to take her longer than usual to get her words out. I quickly got off the phone and drove to her apartment. The longer I sat and talked with her the more apparent it became that she needed medical attention.

It didn't take long for the diagnosis. She was having a stroke. She was sent to Vanderbilt via helicopter. She spent the next seven days in neuro-intensive care. Then another four weeks in a rehab facility, where she worked and fussed and fussed and worked some more until they got her well enough to return home. Then with four more weeks of home health, she was able to live on her own again. The only drawback for her was that she was no longer able to drive. That was a small price to pay, considering what the results could have been.

One of the most important things I've learned from this experience is just how subtle stroke symptoms can be. In many cases they are almost undetectable. Fortunately for Mom, we caught it in time. The brain damage would have been much worse had she not gotten the medical attention she needed as quickly as she did.

I think maybe the reason I picked up on the symptoms so quickly was that I called her every morning and had become more accustomed to her behavior patterns. People, this is important. Take the time to listen to the older folks in your life. You won't have them forever.

The Rat Race

Let all bitterness, and wrath, and anger, and clamor, and evil speaking, be put away from you, with all malice: And be ye kind one to another, tenderhearted, forgiving one another, even as God for Christ's sake hath forgiven you.

Ephesians 4:31–32

All those years of running around like a chicken with its head cut off. Rush, rush, rush. That's all I did. Why? Because that's what today's society thinks we're supposed to do. Guess what? They're wrong. That's not why we are here. We are here to love and to help each other whenever we can. It's not rocket science.

It's no wonder our society has gone haywire. We've got maniacs running around killing, raping, torturing, doing all kinds of vile things. People are so stressed out, they take guns into their workplaces and kill innocent people. We've got mothers and fathers killing their kids. We've got kids killing their parents. We've got parents fighting and killing each other over ballgames and other reasons just as idiotic.

People, we are on a downhill spiral. If we don't get a handle on all this very soon, it scares me to death to think of what kind of future our children will have. There is absolutely nobody to blame but ourselves. We as a society have tolerated the moral decay we're living in today.

I know you are sitting there thinking, *What can I do? I'm just one person.* That's exactly right. We are all just one person. That's how everything starts—with just one person. You start by setting the example. It's that simple. You be the example for your family. It doesn't matter where you came from or from what kind of background. Good is simply good, no matter how you look at it. Just do good things, and before long the people around you will start doing good things too.

Yes, I realize there are some really bad people out there who will never choose to do anything good in their lives. But folks, I truly believe we outnumber them, and if we stick together, we can defeat them. Besides, they will have to answer for their actions someday, and I sure wouldn't want to be in their shoes. How about you?

We are supposed to be so much more intelligent and educated than our previous generations. My poppa used to say, and I believe he had a valid point, "There is such a thing as an educated fool." I do believe our society is proving that point every day.

We need to wake up! And fast! We can't keep going on like this forever and not expect to reap some very serious consequences. Just watch the evening news; I think the current state of our country, not to mention the world, is screaming at us right now.

We have to start somewhere, people, so why not in our own homes? That seems like the logical first step to me.

The Discovery

But seek ye first the kingdom of God, and his righteousness; and all these things shall be added unto you.

Matthew 6:33

Now, with all that off my chest, let's explore the impact this decision has had on my life. First of all, it didn't take me long to realize I had a lot of spare time on my hands. Let me also point out here, for the other stay-at-home moms, my daughter was in school, and I know you ladies with smaller children don't have that luxury... Anyway, I decided I needed to find something productive to do. You know the old saying, *Idle hands are the devil's workshop.*

I chose to explore my artistic side. All my life I have been totally fascinated by the art of stained glass. Its beauty and intricacy simply amazes me. So I headed for the first stained glass class I could find. Folks, I have truly found a passion with this medium. I make everything from stepping stones to church windows. Who knew! I didn't even know I had an artistic bone in my body. When you take the time to explore yourself, sometimes you find amazing things you didn't know existed. God knew it was there all along. I just never bothered to look.

I know in my heart that if I hadn't slowed my life pace down, I would never have discovered this side of myself. If I had stayed in corporate America, I simply wouldn't have taken the necessary time. I didn't want to because I didn't like the person I had become. I had lost the joy of living. I merely existed.

Guess what, folks? We aren't here to merely exist. Our lives are a gift. We're supposed to enjoy them, not just drag through them. If you are in a state of mere existence or confusion, it's time to take a serious look deep inside your heart. There's much more in there for you. Just take the time to check it out.

Your heart! That's the key and first step. All too often we listen to our heads and ignore our hearts. That's a fatal error. Get your heart on the right track first; your head is a whole different journey in itself. There is only one way I know of that will put your heart in the right place. Our Lord and Savior! But you have to invite him. He's waiting on you. It's not the other way around.

Once you've made the most important decision you'll ever make in your lifetime, you'll begin to discover who you really are meant to be. Our existence is all about developing a personal relationship with God. It's not about being a corporate executive, a brain surgeon, or even a rocket scientist. Those things are what people do for a living. It's not who they are. Who you are is God's most precious child, and that's what you were made to be. You were made exactly how he wanted you. Everything we like and don't like about ourselves is a part of us for a reason. So the best thing we can do is learn to like who we are. I still struggle myself with these blessed big hips of mine. I've yet to figure out their divine purpose. But I'm working on it!

I grew up in church and invited God into my life at

a young age. As I grew older and life got more complicated, I lost sight of him, or at least put him on the back burner while I tried to run my own race. That was my major mistake. You see, without him, your pursuit of happiness is never going to be fulfilled.

Yes! There were times of great joy in my life during that period, like marrying my husband, and the birth of my daughter, just to name a couple. But the euphoria never seemed to last long. There was still always that longing for something more. I just didn't quite know what it was. I had a great life, and I was well blessed, but still there was something missing.

Then I found it! It was God. I simply began by making it a point to spend a little time with him every day. Mind you, it doesn't have to be a formal meeting or anything like that. Just have a normal conversation with him. Include him in your normal, everyday affairs. That's all he wants.

Instead of talking to yourself, talk to him. I talk to him when I'm driving sometimes, especially when someone cuts me off in traffic. Sure beats road rage. I talk to him if I pass an ambulance en route. That's how simple it is. Just make him a part of your thoughts and life.

If you will let him in your life, you'll develop a whole new outlook. Don't get me wrong here. This doesn't mean you won't have hard times anymore, because you will. It will just make them a lot more bearable. You'll find strength and patience through him. You'll find misery and self-pity on your own. I certainly wouldn't have made it through my father's death or my mother's stroke without his strength and love to lean on.

This enlightenment is absolutely the single most important thing I've discovered for myself. And I assure you it will have a similar effect for you as well. Just give him a try.

Religion

> And there are differences of administration, but the same Lord. And there are diversities of operations, but it is the same God which worketh all in all.
>
> 1 Corinthians 12:5–6

You know by now that I have found my personal peace with God. I can't leave this subject without talking about my personal views on religion. Before I even get started on the subject, let me remind you that I by no means claim to be an expert on anything. I am, however, entitled to my opinion, and I fully realize that there will be folks out there who will totally disagree with me. And that's okay too. I believe God makes room for all of us who seek him with all our hearts.

I will state here also that my intent is not to chastise or criticize any particular denomination. I will, however, point out my personal difficulties in the religious community in order to explain my particular life experiences. That also doesn't mean I am saying their beliefs are wrong. I am merely saying my beliefs may be different.

As I pointed out earlier, I was exposed to religion at a very young age—as far back as I can remember anyway. Growing up in the Bible Belt, that's pretty much a given. My particular family's beliefs were always of the Baptist persuasion. That is where my religious foundations were developed, and I will be forever grateful for their teachings.

It wasn't until I married a Methodist that I realized I had a few denominational issues looming deep in my psyche. Don't get the idea here that my husband tried to persuade me in any way because he didn't. He didn't really have a preference one way or the other. He hadn't been a churchgoer since childhood.

Several years later, we decided to start attending church again. My first instinct, being the good Baptist, was to return to my roots. That's when I discovered my issues. You see, for me to join a new Baptist church wasn't a problem. Through my repentance and baptism I belonged to that denomination already. John, on the other hand, was a different story.

His Methodist church ritual, or ceremony, was quite different. Yes, he had repented and was baptized, the only difference being that his church didn't immerse him in water—they sprinkled him. It was the same procedure for salvation, just a different method of acknowledgment.

So in order for him to join this good ol' Southern Baptist church we were attending, he would have to be re-baptized and be immersed instead of sprinkled. In my opinion, that was just missing the whole point of baptism. As far as I was concerned, letting that minute difference in doctrine play such a significant role in becoming a part of a church family just didn't make any sense. Let me also point out here that this wasn't *his* issue; it was *mine*, and I was already a Baptist. So I guess I don't have to tell you we didn't make that our church home.

It's not that I was opposed to him being re-baptized, if that had been his desire. I think baptism is a wonderful and fulfilling experience—that is, as long as it is for the appropriate reason and not just to align oneself with a certain denomination. He personally felt his earlier method was fine, and he's just as saved as I am. And I wholeheartedly agree with him. For me personally, the most important issue is being washed in the blood, not the water.

I think it is so very sad that a lot of religious practices today have become discriminatory and superficial. I couldn't give you a clearer example. And it's not just the Baptist doctrine by any means. All of our denominations in the Christian faith have their own sets of rules, or should I say *laws*.

Our relationship with God shouldn't be about religion at all. It has nothing to do with the sign that hangs over the door of the building in which we choose to worship. I think Joyce Meyer says it best: "Religion is man's idea of God's expectations." So as far as I'm concerned, God is—always has been and always will be—the most important issue, not my denomination or religious affiliation.

Think about it. Adam and Eve didn't have a religion at all, and they certainly had a relationship with God. It wasn't exactly great at times, but they still had one. I also don't recall Jesus Christ belonging to any particular denomination either. His goal was always simply to go about doing good. Even though he was born a Jew, he certainly didn't adhere to all of their restrictive laws of doctrine. The simple fact that he is the only perfect man who ever lived and that he would not confine himself to their callused rules and regulations is a glorious example of what true Christianity is all about.

I'm not at all saying church isn't important because I truly believe with all my heart that it is. A strong church family can bring a special kind of support you will never find anywhere else. Church is where we grow and learn. We build great relationships with other Christians there, not to mention worship, pray, and help other human beings. Church truly is a great place to invest our time. My only issue is with the petty jealousy, segregation, and all the other human flaws that sometimes infiltrate God's house.

I can't think of anything on this earth that doesn't have a few flaws, though. Can you? So my solution is to simply go where the flaws are something I can peacefully tolerate. Church isn't supposed to be all for my benefit anyway. <u>I am supposed to go where I can be</u> Amen <u>of the most service to my Lord.</u> That should be our goal every day, not just on Sunday, or in church for that matter.

There will always be denominational issues in the Christian community. I find my peace on this subject in 1 Corinthians 12. My condensed version goes like this: we are all the body of Christ, which is made up of many members. The hand doesn't do what the foot does. The eye doesn't do what the ear does. Simply put, it takes all the members to make up the entire body.

Mom's Deterioration

Blessed be God, even the Father of our Lord Jesus Christ, the Father of mercies, and the God of all comfort; Who comforteth us in all our tribulation, that we may be able to comfort them which are in trouble, by the comfort wherewith we ourselves are comforted of God.

2 Corinthians 1:3–4

Let's get back to Mother for an update. As I write this, it has been some months now since her stroke, and she is still living on her own. She is, however, not physically or mentally the mountain of strength she used to be. I tend to think her condition has progressed to a state of consistent decline.

One of the hardest situations we will face as adults is dealing with our elderly parents. You realize you have come full circle when you become the parent and they become the children. We don't usually ever have to think about feeding, clothing, and sometimes even changing their diapers. Fortunately for me, Mom can now do those things for herself again.

Let me stress here that it is just as hard for them to accept their weaknesses as it is for us to stand back and watch them happen. Mom went through a horrible angry period, and I was the one on the receiving end simply because I was the one who was always there. She resented having to depend on me. She had always been so self-sufficient, and the fact that she couldn't be anymore totally infuriated her.

As for me, my stress level went through the roof. I felt so frustrated and helpless. Here I was, trying as hard as I could to take care of her, and she was fighting me with every ounce of strength she could muster. There were times she would push me to the point of losing my temper, and I would say things to her that were just as hurtful as the things she would say to me.

Then the guilt would flood in. I would feel horrible because I was taught never to talk to an elder with any sort of disrespect. But there were days when that was the only way I could get her attention and get her to stop. Trust me; that was no good place to be.

I have heard of people abusing the elderly. I would under no circumstances ever condone that kind of behavior. I can, however, understand the pressure and stress that might push someone over the edge. In those instances, the wise choice is always to back away and seek other avenues of dealing with the situation. If other family members aren't willing to step up, look elsewhere. There are all kinds of support groups available today that are more than willing to help.

Our elderly population deserves respect and love and never to be mistreated. Their generation paved the way for us, and they more than made their share of sacrifices to provide us with the good things we enjoy today.

Needless to say, Mom has pushed me to my breaking point many times. I can't tell you the times I have sat and cried over having to see her go through this condition. This is exactly what my father was so desperately trying to avoid, and I totally understand why he felt that way now.

Not only has her situation affected my relationship with her, but it has also affected the way I have dealt with my own family. There were times when I just had to leave them on their own because there simply wasn't enough of me to go around.

Especially when she was in the hospital and in the rehab facility; I would spend ten or twelve hours a day with her because she wasn't exactly the most cooperative patient they'd ever had. In her mind, she didn't see her weaknesses. She thought she could walk; and in reality, she couldn't. So she would try to get out of bed, which could have resulted in more injuries, like a broken hip. If that had happened it would have delayed her recovery time even more. And as much as she hated the rehab facility, I sure didn't want her to have to stay any longer than necessary.

The nurses would even put an alarm on her so if she tried to get up they would hear her. Well it didn't take long for her to figure out how to get up and take the alarm with her. Needless to say, that wasn't much help. She simply wasn't strong enough to be up safely on her own without assistance. So that pretty much left it my responsibility because I certainly wasn't going to leave it to chance, and the nursing staff didn't have the time to cater to just one patient.

Anyway, you get the picture. During that period of time I wasn't home much. Thank God for my husband. He totally stepped in and took over everything at home. And yes, even my teenager pitched in on occasion. I would never have been able to pull this one off without their support.

My major source of strength, however, didn't come from this world. When times were the hardest and I felt like I just couldn't deal with it anymore, I always bowed my head and prayed. He always helped me find the strength to go the next mile.

I had a friend once at church when we were young. She would turn out years later to help me find my strength in the darkest of times. Not long after we finished school and were on our roads to adulthood did I realize the reason God put this person in my path.

We hadn't seen each other in years. Then one day I was reading the newspaper. Lo and behold, there was an article about this young woman. It seemed she had a terminal illness and was going to die. She made a statement to the reporter that has always stuck with me and that I have incorporated into my life in many different situations. The reporter asked her how she managed to deal with all the catastrophic occurrences in her life. She replied, "God won't put any more on me than I can stand." Can you imagine being in this young woman's shoes, with her whole life in jeopardy, and having that kind of inner peace? I was fascinated.

I can't tell you how many times that one profound statement has helped me cope. The reason is clear. That is God's promise to us. He will never put anything in our paths that he won't give us the strength to bear. I have that planted deep in my mind, and when those dark hours come to call, I always remember my friend and those words. It gets me through every time. I feel sure that if I hadn't known this young woman as a child, I probably wouldn't even have read that article. See how much comfort I would have missed?

God knows exactly what we are going to need ahead of time, and he prepares our way. He sets us up with the necessary tools to cope with any circumstance he knows we will ever have to face. Our experiences are merely colorful threads he's intricately woven together to make up his brilliant tapestry of life.

From Destruction to Grace

If my people, which are called by my name, shall humble themselves, and pray, and seek my face, and turn from their wicked ways; then will I hear from heaven, and will forgive their sin, and will heal their land.

2 Chronicles 7:14

The things I have been through with my parents have truly been monumental. But to be perfectly honest, they have not been the only dark periods in my life. There is one time in my family's past that I hope we never have to deal with again.

When our daughter was eight years old, she was diagnosed with juvenile rheumatoid arthritis (JRA). I can honestly tell you as a parent that having a sick child will absolutely drive you to the brink of destruction. Or it did me, anyway!

Let me start at the beginning. Everything was going great for us, or so I thought. Great husband, great kid, great job, great home, what more could we want? Then one day out of nowhere, Tait said, "Mom, my toe hurts." Well, being the concerned mother, I asked her what she did to it. She said, "I don't know." We really didn't think that much about it at the time.

Then she kept complaining with the same toe. So we took her to the doctor and got an x-ray, and of course they didn't find anything. They thought maybe she sprained it or something. A few weeks passed, and she still complained, so we went back to the doctor. Still no results. I then decided to take her to an orthopedic doctor and get his opinion. He put her in a cast for three weeks, and we thought that would be the end of it. When he took the cast off, not only was her toe still hurting, now her ankle was beginning to swell. We took her once again to her doctor, and he told us this time he suspected JRA. He immediately made an appointment with a pediatric rheumatologist at Vanderbilt Medical Center in Nashville. Thus began our long journey.

You can't begin to imagine the torment we went through waiting for that first appointment, which by the way, was about a month later. Everything you can imagine runs through your mind at a time like that.

When we finally went for our first visit, the doctor confirmed the diagnosis. She did, however, convey a lot of hope. She told us she would have everything under control by Thanksgiving. Since that was just a couple of months away, we felt pretty good about the prognosis.

Things weren't quite that simple. The medications started. None of the regimens seemed to be having any effect. Mind you, now, it wasn't spreading to her other joints, but it wasn't helping the ones already affected either. You would not believe the drugs we were giving our precious little second grader. Everything from anti-inflammatory drugs to steroids, to cancer-fighting drugs—you name it and they tried it. I can remember at one time I was giving her forty-five pills a week. Then the shots started. Still nothing was working.

I have to give her credit. She was one tough little cookie. I can't tell you the times I cried on my way to work after I watched her get out of the car and limp into the school every morning. She remained an honor student through the entire ordeal. I think the worst thing for her was the fact that the steroids made her gain weight. She got to be a rather hefty little kid for a while. And I'm sure you remember how cruel kids can be to each other. It was by no means a fun time for her, not to mention having to deal with the pain she constantly endured.

We were blessed that horrible year, though, with a great teacher, Ms. Rebecca. Tait adores the woman to this day, and she wouldn't hesitate to tell you that she is her favorite teacher of all time. As for me, she has my eternal gratitude. I will never forget her either. To all you teachers out there, see what kind of impact you can make on a child's life?

I can't begin to explain the emotional roller coaster I was riding. I did everything I could think of. I prayed and tried to make deals with God. I had never felt so helpless in my life. I couldn't understand why God would let such a thing happen to my daughter. I hadn't asked for any of the usual gender or hair-color specifics like most expectant parents do. All I had ever prayed for during my pregnancy was that the baby be healthy. And in my warped state of mind, I didn't see that God had even honored that request. Then the anger set in. I went through a period when I was furious with God.

I couldn't believe he would let this happen to us. *How dare he?* was exactly what I thought.

The harder I fought, the worse things got. We went through two and a half years of pure agony with this disease. I told you awhile back that at one time I had sort of lost touch with the Big Guy and put him on the back burner. In fact, the only time I even bothered to pray was when I wanted something. Well, all this was happening during that period. You see, everything else in my life was going great. I guess I just lost track of who I was and what I was supposed to be doing. I was absolutely taking all of my blessings for granted.

I believe this was one of those many tests of faith we will go through in our lifetime. Guess what, folks? I failed that test miserably. This was literally the lowest point of my entire existence. Sometimes when God is trying to get our attention and we're not listening, well, let's just say it ain't always pretty.

Reality finally hit me. I totally humbled myself and began to take a different approach. I still prayed and asked God to heal my daughter. I begged him to heal her and give the disease to me instead. Anything, just please help her. But I also began to thank him for not letting her get any worse. Because we truly saw worse every time we went to the clinic.

It wasn't long after my return to sanity that there was suddenly a new drug introduced. It had just been approved for kids. The doctors immediately prescribed Enbrel. It was amazing. Within three injections of this wonderful new drug, I began to see a difference in her foot. She stayed on the medication for several more months just to ensure the results. Then they slowly started to decrease her dosages until she was completely off all her meds.

The doctors attribute all of this success to the drug. They say she is in full remission and has been for the past eight years now. I agree that it was the instrument God used to achieve his result because the timing and availability was certainly no coincidence. Amen

I also believe another prayer was answered. Out of the clear blue sky, I began experiencing pain in my feet. At first I would say it was a chronic kind of pain, but now as time has passed, it's more like an occasional occurrence, a gentle reminder, I suppose. For some strange reason, it always makes me think of a rainbow. Every time I see one in the sky, I remember the awesome power God holds in the palm of his hand to control every detail of our lives, including the power to exercise his authority over our diseases.

He's God—our judge—who has the mighty power that could flood this planet and wipe out mankind with one flick of his finger. Then, in an instant, he's God—our Father—who shows us love and compassion by promising not to ever do that again. I think I experienced both sides of his nature during this battle. I am happy to say love conquered all in the end when he chose to heal my beautiful little girl and answer the prayers of a desperate mother.

So now, every time my feet hurt, I look up and say, "Thank you."

Unconditional Love

He that loveth father or mother more than me is not worthy of me: and he that loveth son or daughter more than me is not worthy of me.

Matthew 10:37

My mom's condition keeps deteriorating. She's lost quite a bit of weight, but much more alarming is her mental capacity. She is still capable of functioning on her own, which is a blessing. She still lives alone, pays her own bills, cooks, and cleans her little apartment to some degree.

Her personality has changed so drastically, though, that some days I don't even recognize her anymore. It's almost like my mother is emotionally completely gone. She doesn't see me as her daughter anymore. In her eyes, I'm her jailer. She still totally resents the fact that she has to depend on me for everything outside of her four little walls.

This has been gruesomely painful for me to handle because she has always been the constant in my life. Since the day I was born, Mom has always been the person I knew I could depend on, who would always love me no matter what. Then when life handed me this different reality, well, let's just say it was borderline catastrophic.

Some days are almost more than I can handle. That's usually when I remember my old friend who died and all the agony she went through and how she knew that God wouldn't bring her to it if he wasn't going to give her the

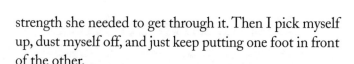

strength she needed to get through it. Then I pick myself up, dust myself off, and just keep putting one foot in front of the other.

I have learned an amazing lesson from this trial. You see, I think maybe God used this trial to show me I had my priorities out of balance. As I said before, I had always had my mother as the security blanket in my life. Well, she wasn't supposed to be that at all; God is supposed to be our lifeline. No matter how much we love our parents, our children, and our families in general, they are never supposed to come before our love for God. They are our gifts from him and are not to take the place of him.

Don't misunderstand me here; I don't believe God caused this awful deterioration to happen to my mom. I think the evil one, the devil, or Satan, or whatever it is you choose to call him, is always to blame for the rottenness that happens in our lives. I do believe God's Word. He takes the circumstances that Satan means for evil and turns them around for good to those who love and trust in him.

Right now I don't know all the things I am supposed to learn from this horrendous experience, but I do know I'll just keep trusting in my Lord. He will not only get me through it, but eventually he will help me understand all I'm supposed to take from it as well.

I also know there are others out there going through the same sort of situations. To you folks, I want you to know you aren't alone. My suggestion to you is that when those dark days come, and they will come more often than you would like, simply change your focus. Get your mind off your problem and put it on the solution. Look up! *Amen*

keep your eyes focused on God

Regret

There hath no temptation taken you but such as is common to man: but God is faithful, who will not suffer you to be tempted above that ye are able; but will with the temptation also make a way to escape, that ye may be able to bear it.

1 Corinthians 10:13

Now that I've discussed some of my earlier years with y'all, I think I'll turn now to some of the uglier ones. This period of time begins around my college days and several more years after. You remember them, don't you? When you think you're grown but you really still don't have a clue.

I am a product of the Woodstock generation. You remember the old phrase, *Peace, love, drugs, sex, and rock 'n roll.* Well, I did my part. I was always on the lookout for the next party. My particular favorite drug has always been alcohol.

There is not enough paper on the planet to tell you of all the idiotic and shameful decisions I've made while under the influence. Some of the blatantly irresponsible stunts I've pulled, well, let's just say it's only by the grace of God that I'm still here to tell you. The good news is, I have been forgiven.

My relationship with alcohol was not only prevalent back in the day, but it remained important to me throughout most of my adult life. I can't remember a time when alcohol hasn't been in my home. Even after I married, I continued to drink heavily for many years.

With age—notice I didn't say *maturity*—it turned into more of a form of social entertainment and a sedative than a party. You see, after a bad day, well, I would have a drink. If I just wanted to unwind, well, I would have a drink. If friends were coming over, well, we would all have drinks.

Don't misunderstand; I'm not getting down on people who choose to drink. I personally don't believe drinking is wrong. But since I didn't like the direction in which I was afraid I was headed, with God's help, I chose to change that direction. For me, the only decision was to put the bottle down. So I did.

Notice, I didn't come up with this decision on my own. For some months I had been feeling God's conviction on my heart about my devotion to the bottle. I think he may have even taken it a step further because it began to affect me physically as well. I had been bothered for some time with hot flashes. All of a sudden, they began to change when I would have a drink. I would have these unmerciful, intense power surges with the capacity to knock out an entire grid on an electrical schematic. Talk about attention getters!

Then one day while I was defending my drinking to myself—I will never forget this—that still, small voice deep in my spirit became profoundly clear. There was no mistaking his direction. I had been relentlessly justifying to myself that I didn't believe drinking was a sin. Drinking to excess (being drunk) was where sin came in. So I reasoned that it was okay for people to drink. That's when I heard his voice say, "But *you* can't."

I don't know why he told me that, but I do know that when I heard him speak to me on that level, there were no other options for me but to obey.

You know, when people think about alcohol abuse, they mostly think of it in a physical sense, like having to go to rehab or through a detox program like all the celebrities we see on TV. I was fortunate enough that it wasn't that kind of problem for me.

It was an emotional addiction. Alcohol had been a part of my life for so long, I couldn't imagine my life without it. In my mind, I associated drinking with all the fun times, as well as helping me cope with all the bad times. Folks, that was just plain stupid on my part. Alcohol didn't help me solve even one minuscule problem. In fact, it usually had the opposite effect. After a few drinks, my problems seemed bigger than they actually were. They really weren't any bigger; my perception of them was simply distorted. On occasion, however, I sometimes managed to bury them for a while, but they always resurfaced with my sobriety.

I finally came to the realization that no man-made substance on God's green earth was supposed to have that kind of significance in my life. You see, it had become an idol. No, it wasn't the old golden calf from back in biblical days, but it had the same impact. We can make anything an idol. Any time we become out of balance with something and put more significance on it than we should, well, let's just say that should be a red flag. Just stop and think about what you choose to worship.

This one amazing choice of not drinking, for me anyway, has really been an eye opener.

Now I don't try to drink problems away anymore; I merely face them. When I stop, look them in eye, and deal with them, they aren't nearly as monumental as they once seemed. There are on occasion those situations that none of us can handle on our own. I have learned at those times to simply turn them over to a higher power, and he will always get us through. It may not always be the outcome we are looking for, but he will never leave us out there alone if we are simply willing to seek his guidance.

And yes, there are still times when Satan trips that trigger in my brain and tries to entice me into having a drink, especially when I'm sitting on the patio grilling a steak. I have found that God's grace has always been sufficient to carry me through without succumbing to his temptations. Some folks can have that drink, enjoy it, and just go on about their business, and that's okay. As for me, I'm not willing to take the chance of going back to where I once lived. There is no way I would risk losing this amazing peace I now enjoy.

The Apology

He that covereth his sins shall not prosper: but whoso confesseth and forsaketh them shall have mercy.

Proverbs 28:13

For the most part, I have lived my adult life in a manner that by no means would be a glowing reflection of our Creator. I'm not saying I have been evil; on the contrary, I have always considered myself to be a good person. I didn't steal, cheat, or do any of the other despicable acts that would qualify me as *wicked.*

On the other hand, I wasn't the most pleasant person who ever came down the pike either. If you upset me, you blatantly heard about it. If I didn't like you, you knew it. And the worst of my wrath would be heaped on anyone who had the audacity to hurt someone I loved.

I guess by now you see that I probably left a trail of unnecessary pain and suffering in my wake. I know there are people out there I've hurt along the way, people I have lost contact with, and people I haven't seen in years. To all of you, I am truly, deeply, and sincerely sorry. To you folks who have hurt me, I forgive you, whether you are sorry or not. I will waste no more of my time on hate and resentment.

Those old feelings still raise their ugly heads occasionally; I am only human. But I am much better equipped now to handle them when they call. Instead of reacting with anger and hate, I usually ask the Lord to help me take the high road. Then I turn the situation over to him and move on. I have wasted far too much time in the past. I have no intention of wasting any more of what's left of this lifetime in the same manner.

You know, the Bible says that God's people perish from lack of knowledge. Well, that was absolutely my case. I pretty much thought if you were saved and tried to live a good life, that qualified you as a good person, and that's all you needed to do. Boy, was I missing the big picture!

Folks, one of the most significant strides in my evolution (this is the true evolution, not Mr. Darwin's) has come from studying the Bible. There is more wisdom, knowledge, and understanding found in those pages than you will ever find anywhere else on this planet. Every question you have in this life can be answered in that book. Let me warn you, though, you probably won't like all of the answers. But the more you study, the more God will reveal to you through his Word. You have to seek before you can find.

The more intimately we get into a relationship with our Maker, the more change will take place in our lives. Don't think this change will happen overnight. It happens little by little and day by day. There will be days you will fail miserably, but you just have to remember tomorrow is always a new beginning if you want it to be. He won't give up on you if you won't give up on him.

God has a definite plan for each and every one of us.

The sad thing is that most people are never willing to surrender to his will in order to find out his plan. I need to point out here too that you have to trust in his plan completely and give up any Plan B you might come up with, just in case you don't like his. That's not the way he works. It takes complete faith and trust in his way. The Bible calls that backup plan being double minded. It won't get you the results you are looking for.

We all have those deep desires in our hearts. One of mine is writing this book. Those desires are not there by chance; God put them there, and he will help you fulfill those longings if you are willing to do it his way. If not, you will never know the level of success you could achieve. You may reach some of your goals, but you can never accomplish on your own the success he can deliver.

Most everyone wants to run the race their way. Well, if you recall from a few chapters ago, I tried that, and you see where it got me. Please don't make the same mistakes I did. His ways are always better than ours. It can be quite difficult at times, but the outcome can take you places far beyond your wildest dreams.

The Buck Stops Here

> And the Lord passed by before him, and proclaimed, The Lord, The Lord God merciful and gracious, longsuffering, and abundant in goodness and truth, keeping mercy for thousands, forgiving iniquity and transgression and sin, and that will by no means clear the guilty; visiting the iniquity of the fathers upon the children, and upon the children's children, unto the third and fourth generation.
>
> Exodus 34:6–7

The one thing my brother and I could always count on, not only as we grew up, but on into adulthood, was the love of both our parents. My dad's love was as predicable and as steady as a flowing stream. Always gentle, kind, and understanding. I can't think of a better example of what love should be like than the one he displayed on a daily basis.

I have told you throughout this book about the amazing strength of my mother. She believed the sole reason she was on this planet was for her family. The Bible talks about the Proverbs 31 woman, who was the ultimate woman, being more valuable than rubies. Well, in Mom's mind, her children were her rubies. And she tried to polish us as best she could so our brilliance would emerge.

For the most part, she did her job beautifully. I mean, we aren't criminals or anything. We are both contributing to the betterment of society in our own personal ways. The years have by no means been flawless, though, and that is what I want to talk about here. And please try to understand this is in no way meant as an insult to my mother. It is simply a part of my process in healing some emotional scars. I have more respect and admiration for my mother than for any other woman on this planet. I thank God every day for both of the parents I was blessed to have been raised and loved by.

Let's get to the flawed part. Y'all know from earlier chapters that my mom grew up not experiencing the love of a mother. So that's where I think some of her perceptions may have gotten a little skewed. You see, because she grew up without a female role model, she was determined her children would never have to know that feeling of emptiness she had to bear throughout her early years. Therefore, we were *sometimes* loved to the point of suffocation.

I am only going to talk about *my* issues as a result of this. My brother's issues are his alone, and I won't go there. It wasn't until I was an adult that I realized some of her expressions of love were, let's just say, teetering on the unhealthy side. Control and guilt were her weapons of choice. I am not comfortable going into any detail that would in any way disrespect my mother, so I'll just say that her way at times was not always the most godly.

As I grew older, I became acutely aware of the manipulation, but instead of confronting the subject I simply accommodated, or should I say, *enabled* her. I was honestly so used to it I really didn't think that much about it. I just accepted her behavior as normal and went on about my business.

As I began dealing with my own daughter, I realized I was doing the same sort of things to her. Talk about a reality check. There I was, turning into my mother. Well, let's just say from this one particular standpoint that it scared me to death. Then I had the light-bulb moment. The Bible talks about this! This is what is called a generational curse.

That's when we keep handing down our bad characteristics from one generation to the next. This was a classic example. I never would have recognized this, though, if I hadn't been on this spiritual quest. Because I was familiar with the concept from my Bible studies, I was much more prepared to deal with this issue. It's like I've said before, folks, our Bible will teach us how to handle every situation that comes down the pike if we'll just take the time to learn. Its teaching is very clear. We don't have to keep handing these bad behavioral patterns down to our children. Just like everything else, it's a choice. As for me, I decided … the buck stops with me.

Don't you think for a minute that just because I figured this one out that God sent down some magic angel dust and my behavioral issues all changed overnight. Oh no! It's not that easy. Recognizing we have a problem is just the first step. Next is when we have to put our work ethic to the test. My best advice here— don't dare try and do the work on your own. You will fail. I started by thanking God for opening my eyes to see the problem. Then I asked for his help in changing what needed to be changed (me). I also asked him to remind me every time I had those tendencies.

I assure you he will be faithful to do his part, but you also have to be faithful in doing yours. It's just like any other bad habit. It can be beat with patience, endurance, perseverance, and most importantly, God's grace.

I am certainly not there yet by any means. None of us are, and we never will be in this lifetime. I'm sure my daughter could attest to that, but I am working and praying that God strengthens me in this area, along with all my other hang-ups. In the meantime, when I mess up, forgiveness is just a prayer away. So I humble myself, grab that forgiveness, and just keep walking it out.

His Call to Serve

The Lord God hath given me the tongue of the learned, that I should know how to speak a word in season to him that is weary: he wakeneth morning by morning, he wakeneth mine ear to hear as the learned."

Isaiah 50:4

It was about two weeks before we were to have commitment Sunday at church. I was diligently praying for God to direct me to the area he wanted for me. I prayed and prayed with no results. So I decided on the angel tree ministry, simply because I love to help children who are less fortunate.

For some strange reason, the entire time all this was happening I kept feeling this gloom over my life. The harder I tried to get close to God, the more gloom I felt. Joyce Meyer would call those feelings evil forebodings. You know, like something terrible was looming just around the corner. I couldn't understand why God was not helping me get past this gloom.

The entire time all this was happening, the Stephen ministry program at our church kept popping up. It was in the newsletter, it was talked about at church, and it was even on the worship screen when we got ready to sing one Sunday morning. Everywhere I looked, there it was, and I just kept ignoring it. I didn't want any part of that ministry. That is the ministry that deals with all the hard stuff. It is the one-on-one ministry for the folks in the congregation who are in pain. Their pain might be anything from illness, grief, divorce, bankruptcy, or any of the other catastrophic circumstances that life has to offer us sometimes. First of all, I didn't feel at all qualified to handle those kinds of situations, and secondly, anybody who knows my personality wouldn't exactly call me nurturing. So I suppressed any thought of going down that road.

In the meantime, I just kept praying, "Lord, where do you want me to serve?" and I kept getting nothing but the gloominess I had been feeling all along. Then one night the most amazing thing happened. I might add too, nothing like this had ever happened to me before. But I dreamed. There was a face in the clouds—not a flesh face, it was a cloud face. I would kind of describe it like how I would picture Moses or Noah or one of the other old gentlemen of the Bible. It didn't strike me as God's face, although the voice I heard was certainly clear and recognizable. It said, "Vicki, it's Stephen ministry," and then I woke up and just knew what I was supposed to do.

I know I told you I felt extremely out of my element when it came to being qualified to participate in that ministry, and I still did. All I could figure was what I had always heard—that sometimes God uses the weak to confound the wise. That surely must have been the case with me. The voice didn't change any of my insecurities, but I knew if I was going to be obedient, I had to trust that he would supply me with the tools I needed to accomplish his task. So I drew a deep breath and told myself what I learned from Joyce. She always says to "do it afraid."

I later picked up the phone to call Ann, one of the teachers for this ministry at church, so I could tell her about my decision. I was, to say the least, extremely nervous. I dialed the number (with hands shaking); guess what, I dialed the wrong number. I thought, *Oh No! Maybe that's a sign and I misunderstood, and I really wasn't supposed to do it after all.* I concluded, however, it was probably one of those other things like the gloomy feelings I had been having all this time. So I redialed and told Ann all about my decision.

She couldn't believe it. It seemed they had been praying too for some women to come forward and help, and here I was, scared to death but ready to go. Now, Ann is not as big a Joyce Meyer fan as I am, but you're not going to believe what she said next. She said, "You know what Joyce Meyer always says. 'Do it afraid.'" It was that instant I knew I had made the right decision. That was God's confirmation for me.

I also told Ann about all the bad feelings I had been experiencing about my decision and how scared and unqualified I felt. She reassured me that was exactly why she felt it was the right decision. We both prayed, and it was amazing. All those awful feelings just vanished. Just like that, they were gone.

I didn't realize it at the time, but now I know in my heart that was Satan trying his best to keep me from making this choice. I've learned that whenever we come to a place in our journey where God is either going to promote or change our direction, Satan will launch a full-out major attack to try to keep us from progressing to our next level. He sure had been beating me to death for those past few weeks. Fortunately for me, I was able to withstand the attack by leaning on God.

After I realized what was happening, I was extremely excited. I felt so honored that God would trust me enough to represent him in such a monumental way. I felt this was really going to be great. Otherwise, I don't believe I would have gotten all that misguided, evil attention. Satan sure was trying to steer me away for some strange reason. I couldn't wait to see why!

Belief Systems

I must preach the kingdom of God to other cities
also: for therefore am I sent.

Luke 4:43

I recently finished reading a bestselling book about a
woman's spiritual journey. After reading her story,
the inspiration for this chapter was born. She took
a vastly different approach. Her journey was based
more on Buddhist and Hindu practices. My journey
has been about seeking the Christian path.

The differences and similarities were staggering.
This stirred up many thoughts and feelings on my part.
First of all, it struck me that there are even more vast
differences in our world's religious belief systems than
there are in our denominational beliefs in the Christian
faith. I suppose I had never really thought about those
differences before because I had never entertained
the thought of being anything other than a practicing
Christian. I know that sounds pretty narrow minded to
you folks of other faiths, but please bear with me as I
elaborate.

It has always been my personal belief—and bear in
mind this is just an ordinary southern woman's theol-
ogy—that the one and only way to salvation is through
God's precious son, Jesus Christ. That is the essence of
Christianity, and that is where *my* allegiance will always
remain. Anyone belonging to an evangelical Christian
faith believes this just as strongly as, say, a Jewish per-

son does not believe that Jesus is the Messiah. And even all Christians know the Jews are God's chosen people. So do I believe he's going to abandon them because they don't believe the same things I do? Not for a minute.

All that being said, here is where I have seen my thought processes changing. We are all seeking God—granted, in extremely different ways and by extremely different means, but aren't we seeking enlightenment from a higher, more benevolent power? I think so. I don't believe God put me here to judge or decide whose method of seeking him is right or wrong. That's his job. I was put here to worship, serve him, and to love my neighbor. Well, how am I supposed to love my neighbor if I am too busy condemning him or her for being different?

On the other end of the spectrum, I also know there are some religious practices that have gone way off base and totally missed the mark. I think we've witnessed prime examples in Jonestown and Waco. Those kinds of sects I believe are Satan's ambassadors, and God takes care of them in his own way and in his own timing. The Bible says we will recognize them by their fruit. In other words, if they aren't producing good fruit (works), that's obviously not the way we should go.

I also think this is a good time to talk about my feelings on the scientific approach to God's existence. Someone I know and love falls into this category. So this one to say the least hits close to home. Because there is no scientific evidence—for example, they can't find the ark of the covenant, or the holy grail, or any of the other many biblical artifacts that science thinks should be out there—they choose not to believe.

I, on the other hand, believe that the fact that they can't find anything is the absolute confirmation. Christianity is totally based on faith. If there were scientific evidence, we wouldn't need faith now, would we? So I don't believe they will ever find evidence until a time when God is ready to reveal his truth to us on a much grander level.

I sure wouldn't want to be in their shoes because they have a whole lot more to lose than those of us who believe. According to science, if I'm wrong, I simply die and cease to exist. If they're wrong, well let's just say it's really, really hot down there. And yes, I do believe in a literal hell and heaven.

Now, back to most of us, after reading the book I mentioned at the beginning of this chapter, I realized the author and I would probably never be on the same page spiritually. And that's okay. As strongly as I feel about my beliefs, I am just as sure that she is just as loyal to her beliefs.

We Christians tend to think we have this all wrapped up in our neat little package, and again, it is my personal package of choice, but I also know that God created and loves all people. Whether we as Christians accept it or not, he sent his son to die on the cross for those of other religions, just the same as he did for us. Maybe he just isn't going to reveal the whole picture to everyone at the same time. So maybe those folks who are seeking God alone and not his son just don't know him yet. Instead of judging and condemning them, why don't we take the opportunity to introduce our Lord and Savior? Isn't that what we Christians are supposed to be doing? I think so. Or, why don't we choose to represent him by showing his love and compassion to those of other faiths, instead of just writing them off as being wrong or a lost cause?

Folks, we can't put God in a box. He's omnipotent. He won't fit in there. Since I didn't understand these other religious concepts, I searched God's Word on the subject, and this is what I learned. In John 6:44–45, Jesus said that no man could come to him except the Father draw him. So is it possible they could be drawn to the Father first? Sure, many people seek God without knowing his son. Then the forty-fifth verse says that they shall be taught of God, and every man that hears and learns of the Father comes to Jesus. That sure sounds to me like some folks might go about things a little differently, doesn't it?

Once again in the book of John, chapter ten, as Jesus is explaining the parable of the good shepherd, in verse sixteen he says, "And other sheep I have, which are not of this fold: them also I must bring, and they shall hear my voice; and there shall be one fold, and one shepherd." That's pretty self-explanatory, don't you think?

But just for clarity, let's look at one more case in point, using the Apostle Paul as our example. He was a Pharisee most of his life. They were the religious elite of the day. That means he studied and was educated on all kinds of biblical principles. However, it wasn't until he was on the road to Damascus that he miraculously met Jesus. So, from this example, you can see that Jesus met him were he was on his journey, not the other way around. He hadn't been converted to Christianity prior to that encounter.

In our culture we have heard of midnight-hour conversions and deathbed salvation a million times. So why is it so hard for us to wrap our minds around the fact that God can, at will, change a group of people, a country, or an entire religion if he so chooses?

Like I said before, maybe some of our other religious cultures just haven't met our Savior yet. I don't know. I'm not a theologian. What I do know is that he said to love my neighbor, and that's exactly what I intend to do until he tells me otherwise. I sincerely believe those religions or denominations that think their way is the only way will be absolutely blown away when they arrive at our final destination and realize they aren't alone.

I would never begin to try and figure out how God plans to bring us all together in the end. But I sincerely believe that he won't let good people who are truly seeking him be a lost cause without first providing them with the same option for salvation that has been granted to those of us in the Christian community. That brings to mind another passage in the Bible about his thoughts not being our thoughts and his ways not being our ways (Isaiah 55:8–9). Who knows, he may choose to do it like he plans to do a lot of other things—"In the twinkling of an eye" (1 Corinthians 15:52).

Into the Light

For everyone that doeth evil hateth the light, neither cometh to the light, lest his deeds should be
reproved. But he that doeth truth cometh to the
light, that his deeds may be made manifest, that
they are wrought in God.

John 3:20–21

I will begin this chapter by saying *I do not want to write about this.* I have been feeling a strong con-viction for some time to talk about something I have never talked about to another human being. If I have learned anything through this journey, it is that if I want to keep moving forward in my quest for enlight-enment, I have to obey God's promptings. The only correct answer to those promptings is *yes, Lord.* I might add too that an immediate yes is best because he can be quite persistent in getting your attention if necessary. I have also learned those things that tend to haunt us only have power over us if they remain in the darkness. Once we bring them into the light, their power dissi-pates, and the healing process can begin. So with God's help, here goes.

We have to go back to my childhood for this, as I recall I was eight years old at the time. My family had just moved to the home that my brother and I would grow up in and our parents would grow old in. It was located across town from our former house. I believe we moved in March, and since there were only a couple of months left in the school year, our parents let us fin-ish our term at our old school before we would have to change in the fall. Well, since both our parents worked and the school buses didn't go across town, we had to stay at a relative's house until our parents got off work.

I don't remember where my brother was that day. All I remember is he wasn't there. The woman I was staying with left to go down the street to visit her sister for a while, and I was left alone with the man. Keep in mind this was a man my family and I loved and trusted.

I was lying on the floor watching TV, and he was sitting on the couch at first. He got on the floor with me and started tickling and wrestling with me. It all seemed so fun through the eyes of a second grader. Then when he saw the woman coming back up the sidewalk toward the front door, he stopped playing and returned to the couch.

A short time passed, and it was time for me to go home. He and I got in the car to head to my home. As he pulled away from the house, he asked if I wanted to play some more. So he told me to lie down on the seat with my head on his lap. He immediately took one hand off the steering wheel, and instead of tickling me like before, his hand went straight into my pants. He began to fondle me.

We drove to the end of the street and turned onto the main road. We had gone maybe a mile at most when he noticed the factory on that street changing shifts (thank God for his miracles). There were people standing all along the side of the road waiting to cross the street to get to the parking lot on the other side. He knew they could see inside the car as we passed. So he told me to sit up until we got past.

After we passed, he asked if I wanted to lie back down. I don't know where that scared little eight-year-old girl found the courage, but she said no. He didn't push it any further. He just made sure he told her not to tell anyone, especially her mom and dad.

For the last forty-four years I have done just as I was told that day. Until this very moment I have never articulated this experience in any form to another living soul. I let my father go to his grave without knowing this atrocity happened to his precious little girl. And I fully intend to give my mother that same courtesy. They were both wonderful parents, and at this late stage in Mom's life, I see no point in causing her the agonizing pain of knowing her child was molested. I don't know if she would truly comprehend or process the devastation of this disgusting act in her current state of mind anyway.

Little did I know that those few moments in time would have such a significant impact on the choices I would make in my future. It would be many, many years before I figured all of that out. I had no clue it was why I tended to look for love and companionship in the wrong people, places, and things. A deep, meaningful relationship always seemed to elude me.

I developed a critical view of what trust meant. In general terms, I didn't believe men could be trusted. I had been so blatantly betrayed by a member of my own family, how could I possibly trust anyone else? Even when good men came along, I tended to push them away. I suppose I was just waiting for them to betray me, just like that innocent little girl was betrayed.

I thank God every day that John had the endurance of a cross-country runner. I fell into my usual patterns with him too. I tried to push him away when I thought we were getting too close. I was so scared to love and trust him. He, however, simply planted his feet and loved me through my pain. Even though he had no idea what that pain was. I think one of the major contributors to saving our relationship was the fact that I saw the kindness and love of my father in him. We didn't meet until we were in our late twenties. I believe had I met him at a younger age, things wouldn't have worked out because I just wasn't ready. That's some of God's perfect timing again.

I used to think a man's strength was reflected in his macho attitude or his physical power. I couldn't have been more wrong. In fact, I think some of those guys were the weakest because the majority of them had no concept of love or feelings. A man's true strength is in his heart. I have been blessed to have had two stellar examples in my life, my father and my husband. These two magnificent men still couldn't heal all the hurt I was hiding from my childhood.

There is no doubt in my mind, I wasn't the only victim of that evil predator, and I think that sickens me more than anything else. He didn't pursue me again, probably because there were several other little girls in our family within his grasp. I was just a child at the time, and I didn't realize he was probably inflicting the same kind of pain and stealing the innocence of some of them as well. Though none of my relatives have ever mentioned this happening, the evidence of lost loves and failed marriages are not uncommon occurrences in our family.

I never got the chance to confront him as an adult. I don't know if I would really want to anymore. I forgave him a long time ago for my own peace of mind, not his; he never asked for my forgiveness. He died when I was in the eighth grade.

I think right now—this very minute—as I try to see through my tears, I know why this happened to me. It happened so I would write about my experience in this book. And maybe, just maybe, it will help someone else dealing with a situation just as vile as or even worse than my own. This one horrific event has tormented me for the majority of my life. I can't begin to imagine the devastation of someone who had to endure this kind of traumatic experience for years.

I can tell you this; if you are where I have been all these years, I beg you, don't stay there and let your experience turn you into someone you were never meant to be. And don't wait as long as I have either. *Bring it into the light*—and let God's love and grace fill your heart. Feel his comfort and peace as he begins to restore your brokenness, just as I feel it right now.

Attitude and Choices

A merry heart maketh a cheerful countenance: but
by sorrow of the heart the spirit is broken.

Proverbs 15:13

Now that I have revealed that deep-buried secret that has burdened me most of my life, let's discuss attitude. Had I been aware of the insights I now know, I could have saved myself so much heartache. I let that secret control my thought pattern for years. What a waste!

What happens to us in this life shouldn't have that kind of power over us. What counts is how we conceptualize those situations. Our circumstances may be hard to deal with at times, but how we choose to look at those situations will have a huge impact on how they turn out. If you choose the path I took, they will eat away at you for years. Be smarter than that. God says he puts before us each day blessings and curses. As for me, I much prefer the blessings.

As hard as it was for me to finally talk (write) about my personal tragedy, I finally, for the first time feel a peace about it that I have never experienced before. That evil power is no longer looming in the darkness, waiting to pounce on me at any given moment. Had I not made that difficult choice—and it was gut wrenching—it would still have control.

So no matter what we may be experiencing, one thing is for certain. We will never get out of it until we deal with it. The sooner we adjust our attitude and go through whatever it is, the sooner we can move past the problem. Just like my predicament, it went on for forty-four years until I finally looked it in the face. *I'm finally free... Praise God.*

This is a good time to point out also that as long as we have a negative or secretive attitude toward something, we will remain in that condition for a much longer period of time, and with each passing day comes more opportunity to develop all of those unhealthy behavioral patterns that can result as the byproduct of our suppressed pain. So whatever your issue, I suggest you face it quickly. Face it honestly. But face it period.

While we are on this subject, not all attitude adjustments are as monumental as the one I just dealt with. We should strive for a good attitude in all of our day-to-day situations. Life is just much more pleasant when we have a good attitude and when we deal with others of the same mindset.

We don't always have the luxury of being around people with good attitudes, though. This was really hard for me to deal with at first. My primal instincts always wanted to kick in and revert back to the woman from my old corporate days. You know the place, where you turn into just as big a jerk and assert your dominance over whom you view as your rival.

One thing that has really helped me in this area is coming to this realization: when most people are rude and inconsiderate, it really doesn't have anything to do with me. They are usually unhappy, hurting people. They are simply lashing out at others in order to feel good about themselves. Then for the most part, my

emotional response shifts to pity or sympathy. I sometimes say a quick prayer and ask God to open their
hearts so they can see him more clearly. Then I try to
remember what Jesus said about shaking the dust off
my feet, and I just move on.

I have to be totally honest here, though. I still mess
up from time to time and get impatient and lose my
temper. The good news is, we have an amazing, forgiving God. When I mess up, I simply ask for forgiveness,
I *accept* that forgiveness, and I put the situation behind
me. I realize in the process I'm still not perfect, but I
sure am a whole lot better than I used to be. That gives
me the incentive I need to keep my peace.

So the next time that checkout line in the super-
market is ten people deep, everyone's basket is filled to
capacity, and all you want to do is buy a loaf of bread,
you have a choice to make. You can let that situation
eat away at you and make you miserable, or you could
take the opportunity to have a pleasant conversation
with the person in front of you. I personally have met
many nice people using that practice.

Every situation that comes along generates options
for the choices we make and the attitudes we display.
Before your feet hit the floor in the morning, make your
decision to have a great day. That isn't always easy. But
with persistence it is possible. We have to consciously
work at this daily. I usually start by not even getting
out of bed until I have spent some quality quiet time
with God. That practice alone has made a monumental
impact on how I handle the rest of my waking hours.

I can hear you right now! "But I don't have time."
Yes, you do. You simply have to make it. It's a choice.

You can either say no to something else and replace that time with God time, or you can set you alarm clock a few minutes earlier and spend that time with God. Either way, you won't regret it.

She's Gone

For I am now ready to be offered, and the time of my departure is at hand. I have fought the good fight, I have finished my course, I have kept the faith: Henceforth there is laid up for me a crown of righteousness, which the Lord, the righteous judge, shall give me at that day: and not to me only, but unto all them also that love his appearing.

2 Timothy 4:6–8

I've known this chapter would have to be written every day for the past two years now. On May 7, 2008, I said goodbye to my mother. It was a massive hemorrhagic stroke. We spent three days at Vanderbilt again, and with the irrecoverable prognosis, we had all of her life support removed. We then moved a few blocks away to a residence hospice facility on a Monday afternoon, and she left this world on Wednesday morning.

The day before Mom died, while the rest of the family was gone various places, I had some alone time with her. I read the Bible to her for a while. She enjoyed her Bible. Then we had an important girl talk. She had been ready to go for some time. She talked a lot about my dad and about having dreams of him coming to get her. Then she'd tell me how happy she was to see him and how much she missed him. So we (I) talked about how she would see him soon and how she would finally be able to meet her mother for the first time and most importantly that she would see Jesus soon too. But I knew in my heart that the hardest thing for her to do when the time came was going to be letting go of us. So I leaned over and whispered to her, "Mom, when Daddy comes to get you, you go with him. We'll be okay." And though we had seen no response in a while, I did see a relieved look on her face like she understood.

Another long day was coming to a close. Since I hadn't been home in days, the nurses suggested I go home that night because they didn't think I would have another opportunity before Mom got worse. So another family member stayed, and I began my two-hour drive home to get fresh clothes and sleep at least one night in a bed.

The next morning, I was driving on the interstate about an hour outside of Nashville when my brother called and said, "You need to come on." Well, I didn't get there in time.

My brother and my niece were with her, and they both said, "She opened her eyes and looked up and off with the most peaceful look on her face you could ever imagine." She went with them that time!

It hurt me that I wasn't there the moment she left. For the past two years it had been just her and me most of the time, and I felt like I had brought her that far. I just wanted to take her the rest of the way home. One of the nurses told me that during all of her years working in the hospice field, she's noticed that sometimes mothers try to spare daughters and leave when they aren't around. I don't know if that was what truly happened, but it helps a little to think so. I do find some peace knowing we had our girl talk, and I told her I loved her the day before. And I realize now too that it wasn't what God had planned for me. I think he gave that honor to his son and my dad.

I think these last couple of years may have been God's way of preparing me to let her go. If I had lost her suddenly, it probably would have not only knocked me to me knees, but it would have kept me down there much longer. My family has been blessed with the advance notice of both my parents' deaths.

I know that for years before my father died, my mother used to pray that God would keep him on his feet until he called him home. He answered her prayer and did just that. So when my mother's health began to fade, I remembered what she had done, and I prayed the same thing for her. Once again, God granted that request. That was such an amazing gift.

He gave us one more special gift I can't leave out. Mom dearly loved her little church back home in Shelbyville. She had not been back there since she moved to Fayetteville. So the Sunday before she had her stroke, all three of her granddaughters and I took her back for a visit. It just so happened that the pastor had everyone stand during the service that day and hold hands as we sang "Amazing Grace." I remember thinking, *Wow! Here we are, three generations standing together in God's house, holding hands, singing his praises.* It was such a powerful moment. I didn't realize that would be our last time.

We buried my mom the day before Mother's Day. I couldn't find the strength to go to church that day and listen to all of the mother stuff; it was just a little too raw. But then it occurred to me; God gave us a Mother's Day too; it was just a little early.

I loved my father dearly, and it hurt me deeply when he died, but to lose my mother has been earth shattering. *My* earth anyway! The only way I can describe it—my heart hurts! I don't think we experience complete adulthood until our parents are gone. To wake up every morning and realize that the two people you have had with you since you entered this world are gone is still scary, even at my age. That love you knew that has always been there is all of a sudden there no more, and you're on your own. No place to run for that comfort and assurance that only the arms of a loving parent can give.

Now, think about that love. I think our parents' love is the best example our human minds can comprehend as the way a physical hug from our heavenly Father would feel. Even with that visual, our earthly love still fails to compare with the love God has for us. He is our true parent, the ultimate Father. Knowing he loves me and that I'm not really alone, even though my earthly parents are gone, is what is giving me the strength to keep walking through this sadness. And I know eventually he will replace the sadness with his peace and comfort that surpass all understanding.

To those of you who haven't known or haven't had the best examples of the love of earthly parents, you have an amazing opportunity. All you have to do is open your heart and receive the love our heavenly Father freely offers. He will fill you with the most amazing, unending love that's beyond your wildest dreams. He is totally accessible, and his magnificent arms are always open all the time.

It's Bittersweet

The father of the righteous shall greatly rejoice: and he that begetteth a wise child shall have joy of him. Thy father and thy mother shall be glad, and she that bare thee shall rejoice.

Proverbs 23:24–25

Once again, I will be facing one more of my biggest fears soon. I had known for some time that my mom would be leaving—I was just hoping that it wouldn't be at the same time my daughter would be leaving home for the first time. You see, two weeks after my mom died, my daughter graduated from high school. So in a couple of months, I will be faced with sending her off to college while grieving my mother's death. My nest will become empty while my heart is already hurting.

I refer to this as one of my fears because it will mean my present life, as I have come to know it, is quickly coming to an end. We all know everybody finds comfort in what we are used to. We human beings do not tend to readily accept change, and I am no different from any of the rest of you in that area.

The way I see it, I have two choices here. I can either let my situation make me miserable and feel sorry for myself, or I can trust that God has me in the palm of his hand and will use this time to open a new door of opportunity in my life. I think I like the sound of the new door opening better, and I'll just focus on that right now.

As I ponder my daughter's growing up, it truly has been bittersweet. It has been amazing to watch her become a beautiful young woman right before my very eyes. The triumphs have far outweighed the failures. Yes, there were some of those too, but that's what makes us who we are. Life isn't about falling down; it's about getting back up. The hard times are character-building opportunities, and if we use them wisely, we grow by leaps and bounds.

I will under no circumstances invade my daughter's privacy by elaborating on any of her mistakes. That's her story to tell. Her father and I made our share of mistakes in the parenting department as well. You see, these kids don't come with an instruction book. It's more like you learn as you go. Just as time changes all things, it also changes the way we raise our children. The same rules that applied to us don't quite have the same function in today's electro-techno world. Don't get me wrong, we still need to keep our time-honored values (God, truth, integrity, trust, etc.). We just have to jazz it up a little so our kids can relate; so they don't think we're total dinosaurs.

Most of our generation grew up in and around our hometowns. Some occasionally moved elsewhere, but they were few and far between. This generation seems to have no boundaries. They view the world as their playground, and with today's technology, it pretty much is. They are full of limitless hopes and dreams that far surpass those of us who are trying to direct them. I have to admit, I admire their fearless attitude—as long as they don't let it change their values and who they are meant to be in God's eyes.

Instill those values in your children as early as possible, and reinforce them by being their example throughout their growing-up years. I believe without a doubt if we take the time to teach them as they grow, they will carry those lessons with them into adulthood. Proverbs 22:6 says it best. "Train up a child in the way he should go: and when he is old, he will not depart from it." You can't get a more direct instruction than that.

When you have teenagers, sometimes their ideas of the way they should go and your ideas are vastly different. If their idea ever infringes even a little bit on those values we've discussed, stick to your guns. Be just as stubborn as they are. At this stage in their lives, you aren't supposed to be their best friend. You are supposed to be their parent, and sometimes that's hard.

Then there are those times you find out you may have been wrong. On those occasions, admit it and apologize to them. We're just parents; we're not perfect. We mess up too from time to time, and that's okay. How can we expect them to step up and admit their mistakes if we aren't willing to admit our own?

She has truly amazed us with her triumphs. We are so proud of her. I don't want to be one of those bragging parents, but since I have pointed out her imperfection, I think it's only fair that I share some of her good qualities as well. She graduated with honors and will be attending Samford University, an outstanding Baptist-affiliated school, pursuing a degree in pharmacy.

I believe her most admirable quality is her willingness to forgive. I have never seen this child hold a grudge against anyone. That just amazes me at her age. Yeah, she may be angry, but she has always been willing to forgive. When she was a little girl, a dog in our neighborhood bit her on the cheek. Her response floored me. As I wiped her tears, she said, "He didn't mean it. He's not a bad dog." That is a shining example of the way she has lived her life so far.

She is also proof that just because you are an only child doesn't mean you are selfish. Her junior year in high school, we watched in awe as she helped her steady boyfriend take another girl to the prom. The other young lady was a senior and didn't have a date. So instead of letting her go alone or not at all, our daughter stood in the audience with her father and me as we watched her boyfriend escort someone else. I don't know if I would have been that generous. Who am I kidding? I know I wouldn't have at her age.

Her mistakes have been minimal compared to the joy she has brought into our lives over these past eighteen years. I have no doubt in her ability to make all of her hopes and dreams a reality. So as much as I will miss her being around, I am so enormously excited for her to be able to go out into this big wide world of ours and pursue those dreams. No matter what her outcome, as long as she is walking with God and her integrity, she will be on the right track. I've told her all her life, "No matter what happens to you in life, you can't lose your integrity. That is something you have to give away." So hold onto it, people. It's one of your most valuable commodities.

I am intensely aware that God is ending this season

in my life, and though I don't know the path he has planned for me yet, I will not hang onto something that is not meant to be anymore. I will wipe my tears, I will press in and lean on him as hard as I can, pray he will direct every step I take, and hope he will give me the wisdom to recognize the door he opens and the strength to go through it.

The Eye of the Storm

Then Martha as soon as she heard that Jesus was coming, went and met him: but Mary sat still in the house.

John 11:20

A few weeks ago, I found myself smack in the core of my pain. My grief for my mother and the anticipation of my daughter's departure had unmercifully slapped me right between the eyes.

I missed Mom so much I couldn't even think or talk about her without crying. The harder I tried to control my emotions, the more intense they became. I kept asking God to help me, and he kept reminding me of the third chapter in Ecclesiastes that says, "To every thing there is a season, and time to every purpose under the heaven." I could specifically relate to verse four, "A time to weep, and a time to laugh; a time to mourn, and a time to dance." I assure you there was no laughing and dancing going on during this time period. The intense sorrow I felt was soul-crushing agony.

The last time I felt pain to this magnitude was when our daughter was sick. But even then, that was a helpless kind of pain; this was different. It was pure heartache. If you remember, I didn't handle the earlier episode very well. This time, however, was vastly different. Instead of turning away from God, I turned to him. And he didn't fail to deliver.

It was during my morning devotional time that the

first phase of my breakthrough came. I had been trying for weeks to put into words the torment I was feeling, but I just couldn't manage to express myself with any form of coherency. Then, all of a sudden, as I was reading this wonderful book by Joanna Weaver, *Having a Mary Heart in a Martha World*, there it was on page 163. She said it beautifully:

> From all appearances, Mary seems to have been contemplative by nature. And while spiritual intuitiveness made her a wonderful worshiper, it also made her susceptible to despair. Instead of running to meet Jesus after Lazarus died, if you remember she remained in the house. Downcast and alone amid the crowd of friends, she had sunk deeper and deeper into her grief, and even the news of Jesus' coming had not been able to lift her sorrow.

That was exactly how I felt. The good news was that it gave me hope. You see, I had not only been miserable in my sorrow, but I felt weak for not being able to shake the misery. I realized then that Jesus adored Mary just the way she was with her weaknesses and flaws. And Mary was feeling the exact same way I was. So it just reminded me that he still loved me the very same way too. And knowing that he healed Mary's heartache assured me that mine too would eventually be healed.

Sure enough, that burden has been lifted, for now. I am at peace again. I realize there are still more painful times to come because I still miss my father on occasion, and he's been gone over five years now. I sincerely believe that losing a loved one is something we never completely get over, but with time, we can get beyond it. And when that happens, that's when the good memories begin to return.

The other phase of my breakthrough came the morning after we took our daughter off to school. I woke up that morning with three words resounding in my head; *it is finished*. There was this calming sense of God telling me I had done my job. I had taken care of my mother, and I had raised my daughter. That chapter in my life was complete. It was time for me to explore new avenues and accept a different kind of relationship with my daughter.

And now that we have delivered her safely to her new college campus, I even have a peace about that too. I realized that we have spent the last eighteen years preparing her for the day she would leave us, go out into the world, and make her own way. Well, the making her own way part is still a few years off. Anyway, she's out of the nest.

We are so very grateful that she is a strong, outgoing young woman. She is out there reaching for her stars. That in itself is a marvelous display of confidence and conviction. Knowing she is able to function on her own at this level brings us tremendous joy, not despair. I would be depressed if I thought she couldn't take care of herself. That's when I would feel like I had failed. So, from all appearances, it seems her father and I must have done a few things right.

I think God used this situation to show me that losing my daughter wasn't the same kind of loss as losing my mother. I will never see my mother (in this world) again, and that is difficult to handle. But my daughter just has a different address, so that's not a loss, folks; that's a blessing. She's still with us, making wonderful plans for her future. It doesn't get better than that for a parent.

Grief, on the other hand, is a rocky ride; a slippery slope that will take many turns along the way. It is a part of this world that we all must face at some time during our lives. It is also one of the most agonizing experiences. We do heal. We just have to do it at our own pace. And we have to want to get better. We can't just wallow in our sorrow forever; that's not healthy. So spend the necessary time in that season. Then get up, get out, and live.

The Reward Zone

Through wisdom is an house builded; and by understanding it is established: and by knowledge shall the chambers be filled with all precious and pleasant riches.

Proverbs 24:3–4

We have spent most of our time together talking about all the challenges I've faced over the years. I think it's equally important to discuss some of the benefits of choosing to seek a serious walk with the Lord. Notice I said "a serious walk" because most Christians (myself included for many years) aren't making that kind of an effort.

Y'all know I grew up in church and was born again at a very young age. You also know that as I got older, I chose a very different path. All I had heard about seeking the Christian way of life sounded extremely boring and restrictive. *Christians don't do this, and Christians don't do that.* Well, I was young and stupid and thought I knew it all. So I didn't find that appealing in any shape, form, or fashion. Therefore, I withdrew from participating.

My standard philosophy was, "I am not going to be one of those hypocrites sitting in church on Sunday morning with a hangover, acting like I don't do that kind of stuff. If I'm not willing to walk the walk, I'm not gonna talk the talk."

Okay, I'll take responsibility for my obstinate behavior, but I also want to point out here that I don't believe we serious Christians and our churches have always stepped up to the plate in displaying godly behavior. Nor have we adequately shown how to obtain the many wonderful advantages of an intimate fellowship with God.

I do realize there are many church congregations out there working hard to address these issues, but there are just as many, if not more, that haven't been successful. I must point out too that I don't believe the shortcoming is intentional in most cases. I think sometimes we just assume others feel the same way we do.

Here's where I think we miss the mark. All the teaching and preaching I had ever heard was how Christians enjoy their lives and have peace and love. Well, nobody ever explained very clearly how that actually happened. And folks, I didn't have a clue.

All I could see was that all the wild behavior I was accustomed to (and, I might add, enjoyed) wasn't exactly the type of behavior I saw from the good, church-going folks. And I really didn't think I wanted to give all that up. I viewed Christian behavior as not very much fun, and I truly believe that most unlearned Christians as well as non-believers are of the same sort of opinion. I don't think it was just me.

What I didn't get was the fact that the closer we become with our Creator, the more he changes our hearts and our desires. The very things that used to appeal to me lost their luster. It was so simple yet so hard to see when you're on the outside looking in.

Let me give you an example. I have always loved horror movies. It all began back in the days of the *Twilight*

Zone and Alfred Hitchcock. Now, I know some of you are young and don't remember those shows, so how about *The Grudge* or Stephen King? Anyway, if it was scary, bloody, or gory, it was right down my alley. I couldn't wait for the next thriller to be released. I loved Halloween because that's when they would show all the scary movies on TV. So I could watch night after night just shaking in my boots.

Folks, when we invite evil in any form—music, movies, etc.—into our homes and lives, it comes. What I mean is that when we leave weak or unsuspecting areas in our lives exposed, that is where we leave the door open for Satan to attack. And I assure you he's worse than a termite; it only takes a slight crack in our foundation for him to enter. So keep your heart as pure as possible by eliminating as many openings as you can.

But now, here's the good news! I have absolutely no interest in those kinds of films whatsoever. And it's not that I fight the urge to watch them all the time. I just don't want to anymore. *God changed my heart.* If the movie isn't encouraging, uplifting or positive in some way, I simply don't have the desire to watch it anymore. He changed me for the better so I wouldn't crave those evil ways. My wants and needs have been rearranged to accommodate my new lifestyle. What a reward that is!

The peace; you always hear Christians talk about really is an amazing phenomenon. You could be going through the worst time of your life, but if you're on a higher level with God, you will walk through that crisis with an unbelievable calm and composure because you know he is in control. Even if it doesn't turn out the way you hope, he'll fill you with comfort and love that's beyond your human comprehension, and he will give you the strength to get through. Not just occasionally, but every single time as long as you put your faith and trust in him.

His love; there is no human comparison. It will never fail to be there. No matter what you do. No matter how bad you act. He is right there, waiting on you to run to him for forgiveness. He will pour out his mercy and grace all over you. All you have to do is ask and then receive. How do you receive? By not condemning yourself or letting guilt consume you because when he forgives, he removes your sin as far as the east is from the west and remembers them no more (Psalm 103:12). His words, not mine.

God wants nothing more than to love and pour out his blessings all over his people. If we seek him we will find him when we seek him with all our hearts (Jeremiah 29:13). Once again, those are his words. So, folks, seize the opportunity; it's like winning the lottery, and you didn't even have to gamble.

Influential People

A wise man will hear, and will increase learning; and a man of understanding shall attain unto wise counsels.

Proverbs 1:5

Let's spend a little time here talking about some of the folks who have influenced me along the way; the ones I feel have had a profound effect on the person I have become and am becoming on this amazing journey, along with some of those influencing today's society in general.

You have obviously figured out by now that my parents have had the most impact on the woman you are getting to know. They may not have been very well educated or the wealthiest people in the world, but they sure had the concepts of love and family down pat. Just to grow up knowing you are truly, deeply, and completely loved is one of the most comforting sensations a human being can ever experience. I sincerely wish every child on this planet could experience that feeling.

There have been all the usual preachers and teachers throughout my life who have influenced me in their own prolific ways. So I won't bore you with every mundane aspect of my childhood. I do, however, want to share some of the more memorable examples I have encountered.

I guess I really should begin at the beginning. Brother

John E. Gant he was a very special man. He was the pastor of the church where I grew up. I told you before that my family was of the Baptist persuasion, but what I didn't mention was that we were Independent Baptist. You see, Brother John E. couldn't be a preacher in some of the other religious affiliations because he had been married twice. That is strictly forbidden in some doctrines. I truly understand that marriage is sacred and that we are supposed to be married until death, but you know, people are human, and they make mistakes. Who am I to judge their sin as being any worse than some of my own? I won't cast the first stone.

I will give you an example of the kind of man Brother John E. was. My parents told me this story many times. It happened many years ago (even before I can remember). It seems that before he became a preacher he was a deputy sheriff in our small town of Shelbyville, Tennessee.

The South back then was not a very racially stable place to be. Anyway, there was a black man accused of and arrested for committing crimes against a white woman. As the story goes, there was a mob gathering to make plans to storm the jail, take the prisoner, and hang him on the courthouse lawn. Brother John E. got wind of the situation; he put the man in his car and drove him out of town to safety. The way Mom and Dad always talked, there were a lot of folks in our town who didn't like John E. much because of the stand he took back then. It didn't matter to him, though, because he knew he stood on the right side of the issue.

This man will always have a special place in my heart. He was not only the first pastor I ever knew.

He also walked me out in a muddy creek one warm summer day back in 1967, where he baptized me in the name of the Father, the Son, and the Holy Spirit. He was also the only pastor I wanted when I was ready to say *I do.* He had already retired from preaching when John and I got married, but as a special favor to me he performed the ceremony anyway. I can't tell you how much more special that made my wedding day.

Brother John E. has been gone to live with the Lord for several years now, but I will never forget this amazing man or all the wonderful things I learned from him along the way. Rest in peace, Brother John E.

The person having the most impact on my spiritual journey in today's arena is, hands down, Joyce Meyer. This woman is an amazing teacher/preacher. I can't begin to tell you about all the wisdom she shares with the world on a daily basis. There is no doubt in my mind that God is using her to spread his message. I know in my heart of hearts that she is the vessel the Lord uses to teach me a lot of the time. Her books are phenomenal, especially *Battlefield of the Mind.* Your war with evil will be won or lost inside your own head. Read and learn.

Billy Graham. Now who doesn't know about Reverend Billy? He's been around as long as I can remember. I grew up watching him, and I might add it wasn't by choice most of the time. Every time he was on TV, Mom was watching. Back in the day there was usually only one TV per household; so what one person watched, everybody watched. Now, I am so very grateful I did pay attention, some of the time anyway.

Another of today's spiritual influences on my life is

Joel Osteen. He is controversial by some people's standards. I find him truly refreshing. Joel's gift is that of an encourager. I absolutely believe this old world could use a lot more uplifting people like Joel. It sure would be a welcome change from all the complainers we run into on a daily basis. He will be the first to tell you he is no theologian. That is not what he is called to do. He is called to help teach people how to keep on keeping on. He has been blessed with a wonderful gift, and I believe he is using it the way he is supposed to, and that's to glorify God.

This next individual has had a monumental effect on today's society, period. Oprah Winfrey. Now, I don't think she and I are always on the same page spiritually. And that's okay. The way I look at it, the Lord said the road was narrow; he didn't say it was one lane. Besides! That's a conversation I would love to sit down and have with her some day. It would be extremely presumptuous of me to judge the contents of her heart when I have no clue, or right, for that matter. I do believe she has made outstanding contributions to mankind, not only spiritually, but monetarily, physically, and emotionally as well.

Most people don't remember Oprah from as far back as I do. Being from Tennessee, I knew who Oprah was at the beginning of her career in Nashville back in the seventies. My mom was a huge Chris Clark fan—the anchorman on channel five news. So, much like when Billy Graham was on, every time the news came on, so did our TV. At my age, I didn't pay a whole lot of attention to the news back then, but when this young reporter came on, for some strange reason, she always caught my attention. I suppose when you're destined for stardom, it's sometimes recognizable even before it actually occurs.

Although she and I will just have to agree to disagree on a few issues, I truly admire this modern-day advocate. The sheer tenacity it must have taken for a young black woman from such humble beginnings to achieve such success truly speaks volumes about her determination. She literally explores any subject or situation she feels can have an impact on our day-to-day lives. How many of us are willing to do that in our own communities, much less around the entire globe?

Discrimination

For whosoever shall do the will of my Father
which is in heaven, the same is my brother, and
sister, and mother.

Matthew 12:50

In the last chapter, I touched on a taboo subject in
our society that I want to explore a little further.
Here it comes, the racial issue. You would think
after all these years we would be better at talking about
this than we still seem to be. I believe that if people
aren't willing to sit down, talk, and actually listen to
one another without all the hostility, we're never going
to get past this issue.

Let's go back to my junior high days, 1968 to be
exact. You are well aware by now that I'm from the
South, and that was the nucleus of a lot of the racial
problems of the day. I'm not going to discuss all the
nationally known incidents we saw on TV. I am merely
going to discuss the ones seen through the eyes of a
young junior-high-age girl.

Our schools had been legally desegregated for a
while, but it still wasn't very well received by the black
community or the white. I remember in my elemen-
tary school we still only had three black children in the
entire school. As long as there was a choice, the black
kids didn't want to come to our schools any more than
we wanted to go to theirs.

Our founding fathers of the day decided to force the

issue. You see, there was still one school in our town that had remained all black, and since getting everyone to desegregate voluntarily hadn't seemed to work, they decided to take the black school and make it the junior high school. Their logic—no one had a choice. If you were going to be in the seventh or eighth grade, you were going to that school.

Well, let's just say it wasn't the happiest of circumstances for any of us. We were made to feel like unwelcome outsiders. For example, I was trying out for the basketball team. I accidentally let a ball get away, and it somehow bothered a little black girl. When tryouts were over, I walked out of the gym and was immediately surrounded by her and four of her friends. Needless to say, I was petrified. Fortunately for me, my big brother pulled up to pick me up, and they left. I avoided those girls like the plague after that for two solid years ... Talk about walking on eggshells.

My point is, it wasn't only the black children being hurt by racial prejudice. Now, don't misunderstand; I'm not saying this in any way compares to some of the pain inflicted on the black population of the day. But prejudice in any form is ugly, no matter who is on the receiving end. I look back now and can honestly say of all the years I spent in school, those were absolutely the most miserable. I had never before and have not since felt as hated or unwelcome as I did then.

Now, after those two years, when we all moved on to the high school, everybody seemed to get used to each other and meshed on a much better level. I don't know what made the difference, other than time and the change of buildings. Whatever the key, I'm sure glad it changed.

Every once in a while we would still have a taste of racial conflict for several more years, though. I recall one incident that really caused problems. There was a black nightclub in town, and it seemed that one of the pinball machines broke one evening. The club owner called the vending machine company. It was a weekend night, and the repair guy, his wife, and another couple were all headed out for dinner when the call came in. They all drove to the club. The repair guy got out and went in the club while the others stayed in the car. No one really knows what all happened, except that the repair guy was shot and killed inside the club. It was rumored that drugs were hidden inside the machine and that was the cause of the rift. Whatever the cause, a man was dead, and his wife was still waiting out in the car.

After that, things turned really ugly really fast. Racial tension was so bad that the police put a ten p.m. curfew on the entire town. I, being a teenager and usually oblivious to things going on outside my own little world, was even astutely aware of all the discontent. I had never seen anything like that in my entire young existence.

It was so bad, I can remember we had a ballgame out of town one night during that time, and my mom was so worried about me driving home alone. She made probably one of the worst decisions of her life. She actually put a pistol in my car and told me, "If anyone tries to get in the car with you, shoot them." Now there's a lesson for you, folks! *Fear* can cause major irrational behavior. Fortunately nothing happened, and eventually things died down and got back to normal.

So you can tell I've seen my share of racial problems from a very young age. Do I think things have changed? Some have and some haven't. Do I still believe there is racial discrimination around today? Of course I do, and many other forms, such as gender and economic-class discrimination.

This problem is by no means solely an American issue either. We have witnessed inhumane treatment all around this planet. One of the worst was the brutal persecution Hitler inflicted on the Jews during World War II. Based solely on his evil interpretations of what superiority was supposed to be, these people were tortured and executed mercilessly. My prayer is that history never repeats itself, and may we never forget the cruelty of the Holocaust.

Then again in more recent years, there was the genocide in Rwanda. I couldn't believe this was still going on in 1994. In a nutshell, Rwanda was made up of two main groups, the Hutu and the Tutsi. In a struggle for power, the Hutu militia delivered a mass slaughter on any and all of the Tutsi it could find. It was a grotesque massacre of innocent people, with clubs and machetes, all because of their ethnicity.

Rockets and missiles are obviously not the only weapons of mass destruction waged in human warfare. Our history clearly illustrates that it's not about our choice of weapon. It's about making the choice to use a weapon in the first place.

So just how exactly do we achieve a more desirable result to this age-old dilemma? Well that's way over this ol' girl's head. I don't know the absolute solution, but I do know we are all God's children. Until we are willing to stop seeing each other and ourselves as colors or religions or ethnic groups or genders or whatever, and just focus on seeing human beings, we will never overcome. In God's terminology, we just keep going around that same old mountain.

Imagine what we could accomplish as a society if we put all this petty arguing aside and worked with each other. I saw that happen for a little while once. It was after 9/11. We were no longer a race, a gender, or any other specific group; we were all simply Americans. Sometimes tragedy can bring out the best in mankind. I believe that was one of God's examples of turning the evil into good.

I've also more recently witnessed a new glimmer of hope for our great nation. We as Americans have one distinct advantage. Our country's basic premise is rooted in the diversity of, "We, the people." And I do believe we demonstrated undeniable proof of that on November 4, 2008. We watched as this country elected our first black president.

Although he wasn't my candidate of choice, I will fulfill my duty as a responsible American and show him the respect that is deserved of the person holding the highest office in this land. I will pray that he uses godly wisdom as he goes about executing the duties of that office. And I'll hold fast to my dream of someday seeing the bi-partisan gap bridged so that once again healing and harmony can return to the land of the free. Our country so desperately needs a new direction, and our people feel a sense of urgency to believe, "Yes, we can."

It is truly a privilege to live in a country that elects its leaders based on the person and not the color of his skin. I certainly believe we crossed a major hurdle by braking down that racial barrier in our political arena. This positive step cast hope to our future generations of all demographic backgrounds. It serves as inspiration in their abilities to accomplish their hopes and dreams, while at the same time eliminating the use of these same barriers as an excuse to underachieve. It truly is a new day in America.

Thanksgiving

To appoint unto them that mourn in Zion, to give unto them beauty for ashes, the oil of joy for mourning, the garment of praise for the spirit of heaviness; that they may be called trees of righteousness, the planting of the Lord, that he might be glorified.

Isaiah 61:3

The dreaded thoughts of spending my first holiday season without my mom had been vastly consuming my mind and emotions for quite some time. Thanksgiving has always been my favorite. Not only was it a time when our entire family gathered for a magnificent feast, it was also a very loving/sharing time for this mother-daughter duo. We had always started our planning, grocery shopping, and preparation in general weeks in advance of the big day.

Mom too seemed to enjoy this project more than most, even after her stroke. It was almost like having my real mom back. Not the stroke victim mom I had come to know and yet never got used to. I always yearned for any semblance of the woman who raised me. And this was the one time of year I could get the slightest glimpse of her again.

But now, even that was gone. I had no idea how to begin to get through this alone. It was a time of great sorrow and depression for me. I really just wanted to ignore the whole season in general, but I knew that wasn't an option. I had an entire family looking in my direction for assurance that our lifelong family-valued traditions would withstand the storm. Our matriarch was gone, and her role was now on my shoulders.

As the time grew closer, I just decided to throw myself into the work in hopes of keeping my thoughts at bay. That concept worked pretty well most of the time, but the sadness was always just beneath the surface. My other means of attack proved to be the magic bullet, though. Every morning, I would ask God to strengthen me for the task at hand and to cover me with his peace and comfort.

He answered those prayers. I watched his masterpiece unfold right before my eyes. My biggest fear had been walking into the kitchen alone. Guess what, folks! I didn't have to. My daughter walked in the kitchen with me for the first time. It was amazing; one generation left, and the next one stepped in. I can't begin to tell you how much it meant to me to have my own daughter beside me cooking that day. I'm not real sure she realizes just how significant that act was on her part.

Then a little later, I looked up, and there was my husband. He had been on the Internet, looking up turkey-carving techniques. There he stood, knife in one hand and a whole page of instructions in the other. That bird didn't stand a chance.

The rest of the family began to arrive as well. Their hands were full too, with desserts and a few new contributions for our holiday feast. The greetings and hugs seemed to last just a tad longer this year. I sensed we were all just grateful to have each other to lean on.

As we sat down for our monstrous meal, I looked around that table and saw my parents' handiwork everywhere. I looked at all of our girls and realized they are as close as sisters. They learned that sense of family during all those Saturday night sleepovers with their granny and pawpaw. Then my brother prayed the blessing over our family and meal. He's not a particularly religious man, but he learned the importance of prayer from our dad. And the pleasure I got from preparing that feast and being able to share my love with my family in that special way came solely from my mother.

God's grace is amazing. It was in that instant that I realized my mom and dad were not gone; *they go on,* in all of us.

It truly was a glorious day of Thanksgiving.

Out with the Old

And these are they which are sown on good ground; such as hear the word, and receive it, and bring forth fruit, some thirtyfold, some sixty, and some an hundred.

Mark 4:20

Surely, as you have been reading these pages, you've been able to see the gradual progression of my transformation. The best way I can think of to describe all of these changes is to express it in terms of gestation. When a pregnant woman feels the first signs of life inside her, it is an ever so slight movement, much like the flutter of a butterfly's wings. But as the baby develops and grows, and the closer she gets to delivery, it feels more like an army battalion marching on with a purpose. It becomes much stronger and more viable.

Our relationship with the Lord grows in the same way. When we are first saved, the Holy Spirit comes to live inside us. We become baby Christians. We feel that ever so slight tingle deep on the inside. But as we seek, pray, study, and develop our relationship, that slightest of tingles turns into a marvelous indwelling that can lead us to the lives our Creator has planned for us. If we are willing to follow.

I realize some of you more mature Christians are probably wondering why I am getting so basic again at this point. Once again, I believe it's imperative to stress the importance of understanding that we don't become seasoned Christians with our acceptance of Christ. We have to work for spiritual maturity; it's a process. And maybe I was a little slower than most, but I thought it involved some more of that magic angel dust. I didn't realize in the beginning that all of this was a lifelong effort that required my active participation right along with God's miraculous gifts of grace and forgiveness. Or it certainly wouldn't have taken me this many years to advance to this particular stage in my development.

So, to reach God's best, we all have or had to start by making a space for him. I believe one of the most critical steps we can take in this area is to just take out some of our old garbage. Many of our attitudes and personality traits come from our past. If we didn't have the best of beginnings or life experiences along the way, we may have developed some pretty unhealthy characteristics.

Those ugly traits have grown over the years from seeds that may have been sown as far back as our childhood in some instances. Those bad seeds developed the root systems that anchor our behavior patterns deep in our souls. How do we break their hold? The answer is simple, but the task is arduous. Those bad seeds and their entire root systems have to be completely uprooted.

You've seen my examples of facing some of my demons all through these chapters. It's difficult. It's hard work. But it is also the only way to break free from their grip. The good news is, God doesn't get in a hurry. He gives us as much time as we need because he already knows how many times we are going to fail before we finally reach his desired result. We are never a surprise to him. The best thing we can do is to stop beating ourselves up when we mess up. God doesn't, so neither should we. Our part is to repent, learn from our mistakes, and move on.

I truly believe the only way to finally rid ourselves of that old plant life that's holding us back is to break up our ground and put down new seed; the good stuff this time. Just like a farmer planting his crops, we must sow. Then wait. Our seeds must germinate and grow before we will ever reap the benefits of our labor. It took time to develop all those bad root systems, and it is also going to take time to develop the good root systems.

One of my favorite ways for weeding out bad behavior is by replacing it with something new. By doing that, I'm not creating a void that craves whatever it is I lost. Like when negative thoughts pop in my head, I've learned to immediately recognize them and replace them with something positive. Or if something negative comes out of my mouth, I follow whatever I said with, "but," and then turn it around. For example, "I sure have gained a lot of weight lately; but I am starting a new exercise program today that will get me right back down to my normal size." See how that turned a negative statement to a positive conclusion?

The Bible says life and death are in the power of the tongue. That means our words are our seeds too, and whatever we say about ourselves is what we will see manifest down the road. So be very careful how you talk to and about yourself.

Another tactic I've learned is that when I am feeling down or I tend to want to worry about something, if I'll just get out and do something for someone else, it not only renews my mind, but it also makes me feel better about myself. Then there is an added bonus; I've also just planted one of those good seeds we've been talking about. And like I've said before, whatever we plant in life is also what we are going to reap.

When I finally realized I have access to a thriving supply of seeds every day, it was truly a light-bulb moment. My logic had always been, "What can I do? I'm just a simple southern woman." *Wrong!* We are all walking, talking seedpods. Our time is a seed. Our money is a seed. Our kindness is a seed. Our encouragement is a seed. Any good deed we can do on any level is a seed.

One Sunday afternoon as I was driving home, traffic had slowed a bit, and I could see up ahead that an elderly couple had pulled over into the center lane with car trouble. My first thought was, *I should stop.* I didn't have a clue about mechanics, but I thought maybe I could call someone for them or take them somewhere. Before I could even think about changing lanes, it looked like the parting of the Red Sea. I counted five pickup trucks pulling over to the shoulder from both directions. Men were jumping out everywhere to help those old folks. It literally brought tears to my eyes to witness God's goodness in his people. I can't express how comforted I felt just knowing I live in the same community with such fine men. There were seeds being sown by the handful that day.

If you give the man putting the new roof on your house a cup of cold water to drink, that's a seed. If you give the old lady your chair at the doctor's office, that's a seed. If you have mercy on that cold, wet, stray dog on the side of the road, well that's a seed too. If you just take the time to look around, you can leave a trail of seeds everywhere you go. You have a never-ending supply; now get those seeds in the ground, people, so your fruit can abound.

I might point out here too that it doesn't just have to be about helping people either. Your integrity is a seed as well. One of my particular pet peeves is pulling into a parking space and seeing a shopping cart right there just ready to put a big ol' ding in my car. When shoppers take the time to put their carts back where they belong instead of leaving them in the middle of the parking lot, they plant a seed. The stores are kind enough to furnish and let us use their property. The least we can do is return it to its rightful place. How would you feel if someone borrowed your property and left it in the middle of the street? You wouldn't want to let them use it anymore, would you? People of excellence return things in at least the same or better condition, simply because it is the right thing to do.

Everyone has to develop their own techniques for weeding out those old roots and broadcasting their new seeds. But one thing's for sure, there won't be much room for new crops until those old ones are discarded. And that's a uniquely individual task.

Every Christian who seeks maturity has to face things he would rather not. We simply have to put our trust in the Holy Spirit. Though his pace is not always as fast as we would like, he will always guide us through the process at a pace he knows we can handle. And remember, he sees the big picture while we just see the next step. So be patient with yourself. Waiting for your harvest is always the hardest part. But I promise you, it will come.

Pain Isn't Always Bad

They that be whole need not a physician, but they that are sick. But go ye and learn what that meaneth, I will have mercy, and not sacrifice: for I am not come to call the righteous, but the sinners to repentance.

Matthew 9:12–13

All the hard times we have to face in our lifetime don't just happen by chance. There is always a purpose. God will always show us something productive from the evil that affects us when we are a part of his family. If we approach our bad experiences as learning opportunities, we can use those same circumstances to help others. That makes their purpose divine.

God's children never have to be ashamed or embarrassed by their pasts, no matter how bad. Those ugly experiences helped make us who we are. If they weren't meant to be a part of us, God wouldn't have let them happen. If the bad things you have read about so far hadn't happened to me, I wouldn't be writing this book. Even though they were terrible at the time, I am now grateful for the blessings that have followed. Losing my job actually turned out to be one of the best gifts I've ever received.

Our pain can actually be the instrument God uses to catapult us to our destiny. I've noticed over the years that some of the most creative and productive people in the Lord's army are the ones who dealt with some of the most horrific circumstances. And those people who required the most grace and forgiveness tend to have the most fascinating testimonies.

To those of you who don't think you have an interesting testimony, congratulations. That means you or your predecessors must have gotten a lot of it right without having to be slapped upside the head. You weren't near as stubborn or rebellious as the rest of us. Wow! What a glowing testimony that is.

As for the rowdy crowd, your importance is paramount. You can be one of the most strategic weapons in God's arsenal. You may have been a little slower out of the starting blocks, but the insight you accumulated is priceless. Then just watch out. Talk about some mighty warriors!

Empathy is all about feeling someone's pain right along with them. That can't possibly be as easy for someone who hasn't walked a similar path. Who could understand the pain of addiction better than a former addict? Try as we might to comfort someone who has lost a loved one, or is living with a terminal illness, or whatever the circumstance, we will never totally understand those emotions as well as someone who has been there.

The Bible clearly illustrates that sometimes the more afflicted we have been, the more God can use us for his kingdom work. Just look at the crowd Jesus hung around. Some of them had some pretty serious issues. Peter denied even knowing him, Judas betrayed him, and he had to cast seven demons out of Mary Magdalene. Now, tell me she didn't have problems!

These people were Jesus's most trusted companions. But it's like our Savior, the Great Physician, said, "If you aren't sick, you don't need a doctor."

Then in the Old Testament, David was an adulterer and a murderer. Moses was also a murderer and had a speech impediment. Jacob was a liar and a thief. In spite of their sins and flaws, God used them to be some of his most powerful leaders. And he does the same thing today with us.

So don't bury your mistakes. Embrace the opportunities they bring. Learn from them and use them to help others. When you do, that affords God the benefit of using you in a physical sense as one of his personal representatives. Your work couldn't be more important, no matter what your occupation in this world.

Nathanael

Jesus saw Nathanael coming to him, and saith of him, Behold an Israelite indeed, in whom is no guile!

John 1:47

Once again, I touched on a subject in the last chapter that I think needs further consideration. Can you imagine what it would feel like if Jesus made the same kind of statement about us that he made about Nathanael? I know I can't! I certainly haven't earned that right, but there are many Christians out there who have. There are many Christians who have dedicated their entire lives to seeking the road less traveled. And they should certainly be celebrated.

I believe Nathanael is our example of those Christians who have been devoted to seeking the Messiah all along. Though skeptical at first that any good thing could come out of Nazareth, at Philip's request to "come and see," he did so willingly. And upon his arrival, he truly did "come and see." Jesus responded with, "Nathanael is a true Israelite." He needed no conversion experience to change him and put him on the right path. Nathanael recognized Jesus as the Son of God immediately.

It seems Nathanael was the complete opposite of our Old Testament friend Jacob. Jacob had to experience a total conversion from his old materialistic ways. If you recall, Jacob wrestled all night before finally yielding to the power of almighty God; but once he submitted, God changed his name to Israel (Genesis 32:24–28). He didn't become a *true* Israelite until that experience.

I think the vast majority of us belong in the same category with Jacob. But the rarest gems are the Nathanaels. They are some of our most precious jewels. I think it is quite fitting that we don't know very much about this disciple. He never displayed any of the grandstanding tactics we've seen from many of the others. He quietly plugged along. Just like when Peter jumped out of the boat to meet Jesus on shore after returning from their fishing trip (John 21:1–14); Nathanael stayed in the boat, laboring to bring the catch to shore. No hoopla; he was the dutiful servant.

It's much the same with many of our consistently faithful brothers and sisters today. Their lack of fanfare in the day-to-day service of our Lord is truly astounding. I'm talking about those Christians who year after year are deep in the trenches, diligently doing the Lord's work without seeking the least bit of attention for themselves. They have always bestowed all the honor and glory to God. These Christians are his most loyal disciples. They have displayed their advanced wisdom, knowledge, and understanding simply because they actually got it and pursued it from the get-go. No extraordinary conversion tactics were necessary.

It truly amazes me that many of these Nathanaels think of themselves as boring. That's not what the rest of us see. So please, don't ever sell yourselves short and think you are uninteresting or insignificant. You have always been the ones who kept rowing the boat to shore while many of us literally jumped ship. Your consistency is beyond extraordinary. I know I stand in awe of your unwavering constitution. How wonderful to have understood and served our Lord for a lifetime. My hat's off to you, folks! It is truly my privilege and honor to be in your presence, to learn from your example, and to serve our Savior at your side. Thank you!

Return

I say unto you, that likewise joy shall be in heaven over one sinner that repenteth, more than over ninety and nine just persons, which need no repentance.

Luke 15:7

You already know I went through a period in my life when I found myself angry with God. You also know it occurred while we were dealing with a prolonged illness with our daughter and during a time when I wasn't walking the walk I should have been.

I've struggled over the years to understand how I got so far off track and allowed myself to react in that manner. I was quite often ashamed of myself for behaving that way and was many times embarrassed to admit I had committed such a heinous crime.

Then one night, with a small group of people, it came full circle for me. One of the men in the group— I'll call him Joe—mentioned how he had a hard time dealing with people who are mad at God. He explained how he just wanted to ask them, "Who do you think you are?" I tend to think that was probably his socially acceptable way of saying he really just wanted to unload on them for having such a blatant disrespect for God.

There it was! My source of shame and embarrassment was being publicly validated. From out of nowhere, I suddenly felt my hand sheepishly going up and admitting that I had been in that same boat before. For a few seconds, you could have heard a pin drop in that room. Then Joe just kept right on going. Now, he didn't say anything I hadn't already thought myself, but to hear it out of someone else's mouth just really hit home.

I tried as best I could to explain, but Joe just didn't seem to hear a word I said. He had his own preconceived opinion, and that was the only thought process he was willing to entertain. The conversation ended rather quickly, but my mind just kept churning. So I asked God to help me finally understand my feelings and to teach me the lesson I needed to learn from my past behavior.

It still never ceases to amaze me when the Holy Spirit brings his revelation. The next morning as I began my devotion time, scripture just seemed to jump off the page at me.

> What man of you, having an hundred sheep, if he loose one of them, doth not leave the ninety and nine in the wilderness, and go after that which is lost, until he find it? And when he hath found it, he layeth it on his shoulders, rejoicing. And when he cometh home, he calleth together his friends and neighbors, saying unto them, Rejoice with me; for I have found my sheep which was lost.
>
> Luke 15:4–6

Deep in my spirit, I knew God was telling me that for us to be angry with our lost sheep or people is missing the entire point of Jesus's ministry. He did not come for the righteous; he came to call the sinners to repentance. I was one of those sheep that had gone astray and needed to repent. He used that time in my life to bring me back home. And heaven rejoiced.

But his lesson didn't stop there. As I continued reading in that same chapter, Jesus told the parable of the prodigal son (Luke 15:11–32). Instead of my usual focus on the wayward son, I felt a strong emphasis on his brother this time. He was angry and refused to come celebrate his brother's return. In his eyes he was the better of the two; he was the self-righteous brother. This brother couldn't see that he had been enjoying the fruits of his father's labor as well; he just stayed home and did it. He had access to everything the father owned.

The wayward brother had suffered hardship that eventually brought him to repentance, which brought tremendous joy to his father. He had been guilty of outwardly rejecting his father's way by physically going off and living frivolously. But his brother had been just as guilty of inwardly rejecting his father's way by not accepting the lost sheep back into the fold. Sin is sin, folks! One brother's sin wasn't any worse than the other.

So when we look at someone who is mad at God with disapproval or disgust, we need to stop and take a good long look in the mirror. I'm sure some of our own sins just might be reflected back. I think one of the most important points we need to remember when dealing with someone who is angry with God is this: their anger *is a cause for hope.* It may mean that somewhere deep in the recesses of their mind, they still believe in God's power, or there would be no point to their anger. They have to believe in God to be mad at God.

Maybe God didn't stop something bad from happening in their life. Or maybe he didn't answer their prayer the way they wanted him too. Whatever their reason may be for being in such a miserable state, it's pretty obvious they haven't gotten past it yet. Just like when I was angry, nothing anybody said or did changed a thing. It wasn't until God was ready to reel me in that I came to my senses and repented. And it will be the same with them too. We're not the potter, people, God is. So we need to stop trying to mold the vessel.

I guess the appropriate question at this point would be, Who do we think we are? We are not our brother's keeper. God is God. He doesn't need us to point out our brother's faults. Neither does he need us to come to his defense. When we mere humans try to defend our almighty God, we are, in essence, insulting his authority and ability. We are guilty of not accepting our Father's way of handling his lost sheep. Just like with me, he may actually be using their pain as the very instrument that brings our wayward family member back home.

What God needs from us is for us to be his helping hands of hope, compassion, and understanding, reaching out to support our fallen brothers and sisters so they can see his love light in our eyes, instead of that hideous reflection that's been staring back at them in the mirror every morning. They are obviously walking through some sort of hell on earth. The last thing they need is for us to fan the flames with our self-righteous indignation. We have not been appointed their judge and jury. God will redeem his child when he is ready, and in his own timing. And he expects us to be ready to *rejoice* and *celebrate* over each and every one's return.

The Quiet Warrior

She is not afraid of the snow for her household:
for all her household are clothed in scarlet.

Proverbs 31:21

This past Sunday was Mother's Day. I still found it quite difficult since it marked a year to the day that we buried my mother. I did take comfort in the fact that it brought my daughter home from college for the weekend, though. It always warms my heart to get that big hug when she walks in the door. I don't think anything feels better to a mom.

I don't know why it has taken me this long to recognize another one of Mom's examples of phenomenal courage. Could it be that we don't fully appreciate many of our blessings until they are gone? All those years ago, while I was living such a sinful life, there was a prayer warrior in my corner, fighting as hard as she could for me.

My soul was destitute at the time. Every fiber of my being was diseased and crippled. Not physically sick, but emotionally wounded. I was totally incapable of seeing, much less being grateful for, even the slightest glimmer of God's goodness around me. Life had dealt some tough blows and had long since quenched the flame that used to illuminate my spirit.

On occasion, Mom would ask if I'd like to go to church with her. I always refused for one reason or another. But I know she never stopped hoping and praying that someday I would come around. I believe I am reaping the benefit of all those years of prayer. Had it not been for her determination never to give up on me, well, I don't know that I'd be here enjoying all of God's abundance right now.

She was the unsung hero who stood quietly in the background, pleading my case to the merciful God she loved, worshiped, and adored. Prayer after prayer she sent up to our Lord and Savior in hopes of saving me from myself and Satan's grip.

I'm sure there were many times she felt like throwing up her hands in disgust and giving up. But she never did. She stayed the course. She stood immovable in Satan's face and fought for her child. Our generation should step up and do the same. The world our children are living in today is even more treacherous. There are evil pitfalls at every turn, and they don't stand a chance without our help.

We have all too often turned a blind eye or at least given in and accepted a lot of immoral behavior today. I am just as guilty as anybody. Here's an example for you; when our daughter was young and wanted to listen to all the popular rap music of the day, I thought if I bought the edited versions, I was doing a good job. Wrong! The innuendos are still there. They aren't slow; they know what it means. I should never have allowed that garbage in my home.

You know what they say about hindsight being 20/20. I see my mistake now, and deep down I even saw it then, but I just caved at the time because all I heard was "Everybody else is doing it."

"Everybody else is doing it" has absolutely no business in our vocabulary. Folks, when we tolerate certain kinds of behavior, our kids see that as condoning it. What is that teaching them?

Instead of standing defiantly in Satan's face like my mom did, I actually opened the door and invited him in. And that is exactly what we are all doing any time we compromise with immorality or evil. There is no straddling the fence. We need to choose one side or the other.

My mom tried as best she could to keep me on the right path. But I didn't listen. I chose the wrong side of the fence for many years. And it all started with just a few compromises here and there. I kept opening the door wider and wider for Satan, and before I knew it, he had an entire band of demons wreaking havoc all over my life.

Moms, get up and defend your children. I can't think of anything fiercer in the animal kingdom than a mama bear defending her cubs. Animals instinctively battle for their young. We should be no different. All of us who are blessed with the awesome responsibility of raising kids will stand before our Maker someday and give an account of our parenting skills, or in many cases, lack thereof. Do you want to be the quiet warrior or the doorman for Satan?

I am happy to say, Mom lived to see her disobedient, rebellious daughter return to the arms a loving, forgiving God. That is probably one of the most comforting thoughts I have when I think of her now. It actually brings a smile to my face as I picture her anxiously waiting to hear our Lord say, "Well done, my good and faithful servant." (Matthew 25:23).

Learning to Follow

Verily, verily, I say unto thee, When thou wast young, thou girdest thyself, and walkedst whither thou wouldest: but when thou shalt be old, thou shalt stretch forth thy hands, and another shall gird thee, and carry thee whither thou wouldest not. This spake he, signifying by what death he should glorify God. And when he had spoken this, he saith to him, Follow me.

John 21:18–19

I was riding in the car with my daughter the other day and became acutely aware of how uncomfortable I had become being the passenger instead of the driver. It wasn't that she was driving recklessly in any way; on the contrary, she is a pretty good little driver. It was simply that uneasy feeling we get sometimes when we aren't in control.

This rationale would also explain some of my mother's volatile behavioral patterns the last few years of her life. She had always been the leader in our relationship, and all of a sudden our roles had been reversed. And just like my uneasy reaction in the car with my daughter, she wasn't comfortable having to follow her daughter's lead either.

Some Christians tend to react in the same manner with our Lord and Savior. We eagerly accept his role as Savior; it's the Lord part that gives us the most trouble. And I'm sorry to say that many Christians never figure that part out. I believe that shortfall may in part stem from not spending enough time in God's Word. Just like when we buy a new car, there is always an operating manual in the glove compartment. God did the same thing for us. That magnificent book with the onionskin paper and red letters is critical for our success. If we are ever going to find our true purpose in life and receive God's best, we have to be willing to relinquish our lead and learn to follow his instructions.

It's only by developing a servant's heart, one that truly desires to please him and not man, that enables us to fulfill our destiny. One of the hardest things for our human minds to grasp is the fact that God's economy is the complete opposite of ours. His world is all about faith. In other words, you have to believe *first,* and then he will reveal himself to you. If you are waiting on God to prove himself first, you'll be waiting a long, long, time.

He has a magnificent plan for each and every one of us, but the only way to get there is to follow. It's giving up our control and trusting him. You know, if you think about it, that takes the pressure off. When we worry and struggle over certain decisions, well, that's us trying to run things again. But when we study God's Word and learn his principles, we eliminate a lot of our cause for stress. Then if we actually base our decisions on what we have learned, we can't go wrong. You will never find a more secure place on this planet than walking smack in middle of God's will. It doesn't get better than that. And you can rest assured that he will never lead you anywhere that he will not give you the grace to go.

There are a couple of big stumbling blocks in this area that can trip us up if we aren't careful, though. The first is that when we see how God is blessing others and yet we haven't seen the same sort of manifestations in our own lives. That's when we need to watch out for that big green-eyed monster called jealousy. Could it be that we haven't received because we haven't gotten past this foolish issue yet? I think that could be precisely part of the problem. Let's look at Peter's example.

After the Lord had instructed Peter to follow him, he turned and saw another disciple, John, following close behind. Peter asked Jesus, "Lord, what shall this man do? Jesus saith unto him, If I will that he tarry till I come, what is that to thee? Follow thou me" (John 21:21–22). Now, how about that? Jesus told Peter to mind his own business.

In essence, we are not to compare ourselves with others. We are *all* uniquely individual, and God supplies us with exactly what he has planned for each of us. Instead of us getting impatient and trying to take control, if we would just send Satan's green-eyed monster packing and become a little more cooperative, his abundance just might begin to flow in our lives too.

Then the second area of concern that can hinder our success, and oftentimes is another reason for our delay in experiencing more of God's goodness, is our hesitancy to follow because of our fear of not being socially accepted.

> Nevertheless among the chief rulers also many
> believed on him; but because of the Pharisees they
> did not confess him, lest they should be put out of

the synagogue: For they loved the praise of men more than the praise of God.

John 12:42–43

From this scripture reference, you can plainly see that this dilemma is nothing new. Since the beginning of Jesus's ministry, there have been closet believers too focused on what other people think, or just ashamed and scared to admit their allegiance to Christ. I don't want to get on my high horse and sound too preachy here, so I'll just use a phrase I've heard Dr. Phil use many times. "And how's that working for you?" If your answer is not very well, then I suggest you turn and take a new approach; one of praise and thanksgiving to the rightful authority would be a good place to start. Because seeking man's praise will get you the short end of the stick every time.

Learning to follow is never easy for anybody. We are selfish little creatures who like to be in control. But as we learn to live the Father's way, he will always be gracious and supply us with what we need to achieve his desired result. And I personally believe that if I spend my lifetime trying to follow Christ's lead, I will be better equipped to handle all kinds of situations that require relaxing my grip. It may even help me find my strength to pass the baton to my daughter, when I grow old and gray, with just a little more grace and dignity.

Helicopter Prayers

Rejoicing in hope; patient in tribulation; continuing instant in prayer.

Romans 12:12

I was reading an e-mail from a dear friend. In it, she shared her thoughts on a devotional she had read about using certain things in our lives as triggers that prompt us to pray. Helicopters have that effect on me.

As my mother was dying, our ICU room was located directly under the helicopter pad of the hospital. During those long, agonizing days, I heard that helicopter take off and land more times than I cared to count. With each occurrence, I was consumed with a deep-seated knowledge that the situation was dire if air travel was needed.

My prayers flowed, always beginning with the patient's health as the main focus, and then for the dedicated helping hands that were there to assist. But I also found myself praying passionately for their loved ones who were waiting in the wings or en route with fear gripping their every thought. I remember vividly watching that chopper take off with my mom, and just how *alone* and *helpless* I felt there on the ground below.

God reached straight down from heaven and touched my heart during this experience with an intense compassion for those hurting hearts that weren't actually going through the physical trauma themselves but were undoubtedly in a critical state of emotional crisis. There is not much more paralyzing to an otherwise healthy person than emotional upheaval.

Let me tell you about this one particular nurse who played a crucial role in my emotional survival efforts. I stood in the corner watching while the medical team prepared Mom for her first ever air flight. To actually stand there and watch *Grey's Anatomy* and *ER* play out in your real life is quite overwhelming. To them, they were just incubating and wrapping their patient up like a little mummy for flight. But to me that wasn't just their patient, it was *my momma*. I did somehow find the strength to keep my composure long enough to tell her to be strong and that I would be right behind her. Then off they went.

As they rolled her away, I felt my knees start to get weak, and the flood of tears and emotion just broke loose. Then there was that angel of mercy I told you about. She didn't say a word; she just instantly wrapped both arms around me and held me for a while. It was truly an amazing moment. It was just like Jesus with skin on or something.

Now, I don't remember that nurse's name, and I don't even know if I would recognize her again, but what I do know is that I will never forget that experience and what her compassion meant to me. And I can assure you this woman did not merely choose nursing as a profession; nursing is her *God-ordained call.* Big difference.

To many of us non-medical folks, the health-care community seems to take professionalism to the extreme at times, with no signs of humanity anywhere to be seen. In all fairness, though, I feel we (Joe Public) have to accept some of the responsibility for their behavior. These people have spent countless hours and huge sums of money to achieve their goals. Then in a split second, it can all come crashing down with one frivolous lawsuit. I would probably be a little guarded myself under those circumstances. But I sure am grateful God put the right professional in my path that dreadful day. She was the one who worried more about the human being in front of her than the protocol.

Now, as horrible as that whole experience was at the time, I am now grateful that God has once again taught me a few more of his magnificent lessons. He showed me how to *rejoice in hope* over his true intended nature of mankind by introducing me to an amazing, compassionate nurse in a sea of bureaucracy and regimen. *Patience in tribulation* came when I finally learned to *accept* what I could not control. And last but certainly not least, he showed me how to be *instant in prayer,* with the sound of helicopter blades.

The Itch

Submit yourselves therefore to God. Resist the
devil, and he will flee from you.

James 4:7

When the weather is agreeable—down here
in southern Tennessee, that usually means
when it's below ninety degrees—I thoroughly enjoy having my morning quiet time on my
back porch. It's beyond me how anyone can be exposed
to nature and ignore God's brilliance. When that warm
breeze blows across my face, it's like a gentle kiss from
heaven.

This particular morning, Joyce Meyer happened to
be teaching me about emotional maturity in her book
Managing Your Emotions. The section I was reading
was talking about how "It takes a constant act of will to
do things God's way and not our way."

After reading that statement, I paused to think
about it for a moment. Then one of God's most glorious creatures, a hummingbird, flew up to have some
breakfast out of my feeder. He was so close I could see
every fascinating detail. I remained as still as could be
because I knew if I moved, he would be gone just as
quickly as he had appeared. It was in that very instant
that I felt an intolerable itch right between my shoulder blades. Now, I knew if I reached to scratch that
itch, my new friend would be gone in a split second.

So I suffered through that gnawing urge until the little guy got his belly full and went on his way.

That's when it occurred to me, God had just validated Joyce's teaching. It took an act of sheer will for me to overcome the urge to scratch that itch. And by conquering that feeling, I was able to continue enjoying God's beauty. I think this may be a key step in maintaining a continued state of peace and joy.

But I'm sorry to say many of us live at the mercy of our feelings and emotions. Until we learn to control them instead of them controlling us, we will be unable to experience and appreciate his wonderful bounty with any consistency. I know I struggle with this issue myself sometimes. Occasionally I will drop my guard for what seems like a millisecond, and that's all it takes to get out of balance and go on another one of Satan's joy rides.

For example, one of my trigger spots is some of the parent–teenager issues that can many times cause a war of wills, before any resolution is ever reached. In the beginning, I would get totally bent out of shape. I have since learned to make prayer my first line of defense. Self-talk, for me anyway, is helpful too. Speaking God's Word out loud can unleash all kinds of power in any situation, and I don't hesitate to swing that *sword of the Spirit* at the first sign of trouble.

When we learn to recognize our vulnerable areas, we give ourselves a much better chance at overcoming our weaknesses. But here's the hard part. As long as we are in this human form, we will never be in complete control because we will always have our feelings and emotions in the mix. We just have to work on getting better at maintaining the balance that allows us to keep them in check. If you recall, Joyce said it was a "constant act of will."

Our fickle feelings and emotions are two of Satan's favorite tools when it comes to stealing our joy. He baits us by putting those nagging little thoughts in our heads, which usually results in us losing focus and getting out of God's will for a time. So whatever you do, don't scratch that itch.

Looking Back

Come unto me, all ye that labour and are heavy laden, and I will give you rest. Take my yoke upon you, and learn of me; for I am meek and lowly in heart: and ye shall find rest unto your souls. For my yoke is easy, and my burden is light.

Matthew 11:28–30

I feel compelled to revisit the beginning of this now seven-year-long journey. As I reflect, I hardly recognize the woman who first started out on this quest. She was such an angry, bitter, lost soul, yearning for anything other than her past or present circumstances. She was so utterly stressed and burned out that it's beyond my comprehension how she managed to function as well as she did.

The corruption she had seen in the workplace went against every fiber of her being, and yet she stayed. Why? Because she never slowed down long enough to find out what her purpose in life really was. At that particular season in her life, she accepted those deplorable conditions as the norm. She totally let her environment dictate who she was, instead of it being simply what she did for a living. It consumed her identity entirely.

I'm sure you've heard the old saying, "ignorance is bliss." Well, in my case, it wasn't. I believe the reason I was so miserable in corporate America was that I was never truly meant to be a part of that arena. It was like trying to fit a square peg in a round hole; it just didn't fit.

This amazing journey has taught me that I am more a creative being than one who thrives in a structured corporate environment. Don't get me wrong here! I was a very good employee; it was by no means a lack of ability. But you see, any time we are trying to pursue avenues that were never meant for us, let's just say there will always be a hole or feelings of emptiness that we just can't seem to understand. That's a red flag, folks, screaming at you, telling you you're not where you belong.

I know it sounds like I am opposed to life in the corporate world. I assure you that is not my intent. Our global economy couldn't survive without this form of commerce. I do, however, truly believe that it, along with a few other industries out there, desperately needs to change. I also realize today's economic world couldn't possibly operate by our forefathers' standards, which is a shame. They sealed a deal with a handshake, and their word was their bond. Those days are dead and gone, mainly due to legal ramifications. We have become a nation of vipers that sue our neighbors at the drop of a hat. That wasn't what God intended.

God! Yeah, we've dropped him out of almost everything. And folks, mark my words, if that doesn't change, that will be the downfall of this great nation. We are seeing the results every day. We kicked him out of our schools, and now we have kids killing kids. We kicked him out of our courts, and just look at mess they are in. Just look around on a daily basis; you can't even walk through the shopping malls without seeing sexually explicit posters all over the place just infiltrating the innocent minds of our children.

We used to be a blessed nation. Then we forgot where the blessings were coming from, and look what's happening. We need to do some serious house cleaning all around this country, not just in our corporate structure. It's not too late to change, but we have to start now. How, you ask? We as a people have to stop putting up with all the terrible things going on around us. We have to seek honesty and integrity again, not lying, cheating, and stealing. We have to elect responsible representatives in Washington. The main thing in my opinion is that we have to go back to basics.

There is only one word I can think of to describe the solution to our problems. *Simplify!* That's it. Slow down, look, feel, taste, smell, and touch. That's the only answer. If we are not willing to do that, we don't have a chance.

I'm not saying go quit your job, or anything that drastic. But I am sure most people out there are trying to accomplish way more in a twenty-four-hour period than is humanly possible. So just stop it. One of the major examples I can think of to give you is this; your child doesn't have to be on the dance team, the cheerleading squad, the basketball team, girl scouts, the soccer team, *and* the volleyball team. That's unreasonable. Make her choose. It won't kill her. And it won't make you any less of a mother or father either. In fact, it would probably free up some much-needed quality time. Who knows? You may even get to know each other a little better.

Yes, even you workaholics out there could stand to

shave a little time off your busy schedules too. My best tip for y'all; when you leave work, leave work at work. You are only cheating yourselves and your families by bringing your job home with you. I assure you it will be there in the morning. I do realize there are those emergencies that arise, and that's understandable; but those should be occasional, not daily.

Now for the Joneses! If most of you have to work twenty-four-seven to keep things afloat, then you are probably living above your means, and you might want to seriously consider reevaluating your priorities. We as a society have way too much focus on money and stuff. We simply don't need all the so-called *stuff.* Yes, we like it, but we don't need it. Don't misunderstand; I like my stuff just as much as the next fellow. What I am saying is it all depends on the lengths we go to and what we are sacrificing in order to attain the stuff.

I will point out too that I'm not talking about those single-parent homes who are doing all they can to keep things going. In fact, I admire their willingness to fight for their families and not just sit down and expect the taxpayers to support them. There are way too many lazy people out there milking the system for everything it's worth today. And getting away with it.

We have forgotten how to relax. Everything today is go, go, go. When we choose to operate at that pace, well, it's no wonder we've lost our focus on the important things. I know when I have more on my plate than I can comfortably handle, that is usually when I get stressed out. Then come testy and short tempered. I'm sure that's the way most of you are as well. Guess what? That should be a signal telling us we're out of balance.

We are supposed to be pursuing peace at all times. Notice I said *pursue* because it doesn't just happen. You have to work at that one every single day.

There are those people in the world who had to learn these lessons the hard way. I'm talking about those folks that put so much emphasis on their jobs, money, and climbing the ladder to the top that they ended up losing their real blessings as well as their families a lot of the time. Yeah, they have their money and jobs, but that's all they have. That sure doesn't keep you warm on a cold night or bring you chicken soup when you're sick. I can't imagine how that could possibly bring happiness. Besides, as volatile as the corporate world is today, all of that could be lost tomorrow. Then what?

Again, I'm not saying quit. I'm simply saying, "Get your priorities in order." Stop selling your souls so you can live a little higher on the hog. All that stuff you are providing for your children is not teaching them right from wrong, or spending time with them, or praying with them, or just enjoying watching them grow up.

Look at it this way—if you died today, how long do you think it would take your company to replace you? I guess a week, or maybe even a month. Now, how long would it take your family to replace you? There is no replacement.

Conclusion

And now brethren, I commend you to God, and to the word of his grace, which is able to build you up, and to give you an inheritance among all them which are sanctified.

Acts 20:32

Well, at some point I guess there comes a time to end this philosophy of mine, and now seems to be as good a time as any. So I will devote this chapter to my thoughts on what I hope you good folks received from our time together.

I have been out of corporate America for almost seven years now, and I have been working on this book off and on the entire time. Most of these insights developed over a period of time, not simply overnight. It has truly been a work in progress. There were smiles, tears, happiness, heartache, and much more all along the way. Hopefully I have gained the knowledge I was supposed to so that I could share it with you.

So, as you make your way through your everyday lives, always keep in mind that it's all about the journey. As long as there is breath in your body, there will be trials, tribulations, and tests all along the way. Our job is not to avoid the hard times. That's just not going to happen. Besides, that's when we do most of our growing and changing. Our job is to go through those times with as much grace and dignity as we can so the rest of the world can see the power of God in his people.

And the stronger we become in our relationship with our Maker, the more blessings will come our way as well. It's not all work; the rewards are simply amazing; not to mention well worth the end results. So if you are willing to tackle all the work on your journey, God will take care of your destination.

Don't forget, it's war out there! So put on God's armor (Ephesians 6:11–17) every single day so you will at least stand a fighting chance at surviving all the evil attacks that come our way. Satan is relentless, and all he wants is to destroy us. The good news is that he can't do that without our help. If we stay focused on the right track and keep turning to God, Satan is a defeated foe. Just read the end of your Bible. We win!

I don't believe in luck. So I don't believe you are reading this book by chance. I believe in a divine plan from a higher power. Just as you have witnessed the changes in my life through these pages, God will do the same thing for you. He doesn't play favorites. So if you don't get anything else out of this book other than *there is a God who loves you and wants good things for you,* well congratulations, you're on your way. Now I suggest you seek his plan with every ounce of strength you can find.

I have said this several times. I don't claim to be an expert on anything. I'm just an ordinary southern woman on an amazing quest for spiritual enlightenment. This life is my precious gift from God, and I'll cherish every minute detail of it. I hope I gain enough wisdom, knowledge, and understanding along the way to live out the divine plan he has for me.

I believe in my heart that most people in this world

see their lives as pretty simple and boring. I'm here to tell you that is absolutely not what God sees. Just take the time to look deeper, and I know you'll find it. I promise you there is more on the inside of you than you can ever begin to imagine.

So until next time, may God's goodness keep you in his perfect peace, and I pray you folks become passionate in your search for his best.

Bibliography

Joanna Weaver, *Having* A Mary Heart in a *Martha World*, Waterbook Press, 1st edition, July 18, 2000

Joyce Meyer, *Confident Woman,* Faithwords, September 5, 2006

Joyce Meyer, *Battlefield* of *the Mind,* Faithwords, October 2002

The Wycliffe Bible Commentary, Copyright 1962, by The Moody Bible Institute of Chicago